OL' SWAMPER'S RHODE ISLAND SHELLFISH & CLAMBAKE COOKBOOK

by
Earl "The Younger" LeClaire
&
Timothy "Ol' Swamper" Gilchrist

Original title
OL' SWAMPER'S RHODE ISLAND
SHELLFISH & CLAMBAKE COOKBOOK

Cover image
Earl LeClaire

Cover design
Sonja Smolec

Layout
Yossi Faybish
Sonja Smolec

Published by
Aquillrelle

© Copyright Earl LeClaire, Timothy Gilchrist, 2016

Printed in the United States of America

ISBN 978-1-329-85920-3

Table of Contents

INTRODUCTION

A former food critic, for the San Francisco Examiner, wrote a scathing review of Rhode Island cuisine. Among those scolded were Champlin's Seafood of Point Judith, for its lobster roll, served on, heaven forbid, "a hot dog bun," Haven Brothers, in Providence, for their "impertinent attitude," The Black Pearl, Newport, for its plain-broth clam chowder, and Angelo's of Providence, for the "common" pasta presentation. Ah, the snobbery inherent there. That's why we do not ascribe to giving food critics the power to make or break a restaurant, or to their denunciation of some regional cuisine and exhalation of others. There are enough restaurants and cooking styles in the world to interest everyone and it is my belief that professional critics should concentrate on the ones they like and present their criticism of those constructively. There's enough negativity and schlock in the world without bringing it to the dining table to sink in your gut like a greasy donut. Besides which, Rhode Island cuisine holds its own, especially as concerns seafood.

While this book concentrates on traditional Rhode Island and New England shellfish recipes, it also includes a few from other regions of the United States that celebrate America's shellfish cooking heritage.

When Rhode Island native, Timothy "Ol' Swamper" Gilchrist, of Charleston, developed his, *Gilchrist Shellfish Griller*, he added a new dimension to cooking shellfish. He asked me to help put a few recipes together for his website. A few recipes developed for the *Gilchrist Shellfish Griller* turned into many because the refrain while creating and testing them was the same as that repeated by all clam-diggers standing in the water with rake in hand - "Just one more!"

We hope you find a few favorites here and encourage you to expand upon these recipes and to develop some of your own.

Shellfish lovers - Enjoy!

~Earl LeClaire

I. THE BASICS

SHELLFISH

Shellfish fall into two general categories: *mollusks* and *crustaceans*. Most mollusks have soft bodies which are fully or partially enclosed in a shell, such as clams, oysters, mussels, scallops, cockles, abalone, geoduck, conch, periwinkles, limpets and snails. However, squid and octopus, (cephalopods), have internal shells but are also mollusks. Crustaceans have elongated, segmented bodies such as lobsters, shrimp, crayfish and crabs.

This cookbook deals with mollusks, specifically, clams, mussels, oysters and conch. We will also discuss snails as snail farming is on the increase and snails are more readily available then they once were. We will not take up periwinkles and limpets as they are, for our purposes, of minor consequence and abalone and geoduck, unless farmed, are hard to come by and as a rule available only on the Pacific Coast. We will, however, add one recipe for conch salad as it is a Rhode Island specialty and is on the menu in many restaurants.

AQUACULTURE

Aquaculture is the farming of aquatic animals. Marine aquaculture has been a boon for lovers of shellfish as over-fishing, changing ocean environments and pollution have seriously depleted the supply. Today, much of the shellfish we purchase are farmed: clams, oysters, mussels, snails, abalone, shrimp, etc. However, with this boon comes new problems in the areas of water supplies, feed (abalone, for example, require large amounts of kelp) and waste disposal. As these problems build, aquaculturists, in America, Europe and Asia, are rising to the challenge and are working to solve problems as they arise to insure a continuous and plentiful supply and variety of seafood to the markets.

MOLLUSKS

Clams

Quahogs, Littlenecks, Cherrystones, Sea Clams and Steamers, these are the clams we use in the recipes in this book.

The Quahog, or Atlantic Hard-shell Clam, pronounced *kuô'-hôg*, from the Narragansett word for the clam "poquaûhock," is a hard shell clam found on the Atlantic Coast from Nova Scotia to Florida. It ranges in size from 1-3/8 to 4 inches across. The smallest are called, Littlenecks, the mid-size are Cherrystones, the large ones, Quahogs. Both littlenecks and cherrystones are eaten raw on the half-shell, and used as appetizers in dishes such as "Clams Casino," in clam sauces for pasta and fish, for barbecuing, steaming and can also be used in soups.

The quahog is used in chowders, clam cakes, (fritters), and stuffed clams. The quahog is tenderer than the large Sea or Surf Clam and hence favored over the large clam which is the clam usually found chopped and canned or frozen.

The Steamer is the Atlantic Soft-shell Clam also called Ipswich Clam and Longneck Clam. It is usually steamed or fried. I'm told that some people eat them raw but no one I know. The necks of the steamer are chewy but the rest of the meat is soft and succulent and dipped in melted butter is an incredible treat. The

Atlantic steamer has been successfully transplanted to the Puget Sound area and is now harvested there. However, there is a soft-shell clam native to Washington State which is so close to the Atlantic soft-shell that for many years it was thought to be a transplant from New England.

Preparing Clams

Preparing Quahogs, Cherrystones, Littlenecks and Sea Clams.

Most producers hold their shellfish in seawater to purge them before they send them to market. Some even scrub them. But if the shells are dirty or muddy, at least an hour before opening scrub the shells with a stiff-bristle brush and rinse under cool water.

When opening, handle the clams gently or they will close tighter. Grip the clam with the hinge towards the palm of your hand, insert a clam knife between the shells and press the knife firmly in. Don't wiggle it or the shells will break on the edges. If they're too tight to open or if the edges break, place them in a freezer for 5 or 6 minutes. The shells should part slightly making them easier to open. Once open, sever the muscles and free the clam from the top shell and separate the shells.

Grilling tip: if shucking the hard-shell clam, try to avoid spilling the juice so that each of the shellfish will poach in its own juice.

The retention of the juice is critical to the blending of flavors. Note: if you grill them unshucked the shellfish open when heated thereby saving the natural juices. You must discard any shell fish that do not open once exposed to heat.

Note: Having trouble shucking clams to serve in a Raw Bar? Once again, place them in a freezer for five or six minutes. They'll open enough to make shucking easier.

Preparing Steamers

Before cooking steamers or opening for frying, place them in a bucket of saline water (1/2 cup salt to 1 gallon water; never just fresh water or they'll die) with 1 cup of cornmeal. This will purge the clam of sand and mud. If very sandy or muddy, change the water once during the process. To open steamers simply insert a knife between the shells and free the clam from the shell. Then remove the thin, dark "veil" from the neck. Some people discard the neck altogether as it is tough, I don't.

Oysters

There are four types of oysters, the *Atlantic (or Eastern) Oyster*, the *Pacific Oyster*, the *Olympia Oyster* and the *European Flat Oyster* (often called *Belon Oyster*).

Oysters are also known and marketed by other names such as, Apalachicola, Long Island, Blue Point, etc. These names simply refer to the area they come from.

Oysters are graded by size: counts, selects and standards. Counts, the largest, are best suited for stews and main dishes such as casseroles and fried oysters. They are also good grilled and used for barbecue. Selects are mid-sized and also great for grilling and main dishes. They are also ideal for hors d'oeuvres and raw bars. Standards are the smallest and especially good for frying, raw bars and dishes like the "Hangtown Fry".

Although available year round, I believe oysters are at their best in the months with an R in them. Some "experts" dismiss this old adage as merely myth, but during the warmer spawning months, oysters use up their stored glycogen (a polysaccharide, a form of glucose in animal cells) during the spawning process and are generally watery, milky and not as firm. Therefore, most oyster farms in the United States do not harvest during the summer months. During those months oysters are primarily imported from New Zealand and Eastern Canada, although now we have the *Triploid Pacific Oyster*, which we will consider with the Pacific Oyster.

The *Pacific Oyster* was first imported from Japan to California, Oregon, Washington and British Columbia in 1921 and continued to be, with the exception of the World War II years, until 1970. Oyster seed is now provided year round from West Coast hatcheries. However, genetically engineered oysters, called *Triploid Pacific Oysters* which, having three sets of chromosomes rather than the usual two (diploid), do not spawn and remain firm fleshed year round. Triploid oysters now account for over a third of the total US West Coast oyster production and are harvested year round.

The *Atlantic Oyster* is native to the Eastern seaboard and the Gulf. At one time it ranged from Nova Scotia all the way to the farthest Atlantic waters of Mexico.

The *Olympia Oyster*, the smallest of the oysters, is native to America's West Coast. Once found from the Los Angeles to Alaska they were nearly wiped out in the late 1800's by over fishing. The Olympia is now primarily cultivated in Washington's Puget Sound but is still limited and generally seeded from wild beds, although a few West Coast hatcheries are now making Olympia oyster seed available.

The *European Flat Oyster* (or sometimes referred to as *Belon* after the area in France where it was first cultivated) is also being farmed in the United States. The European is a little smaller than the Atlantic and Pacific oyster and is considered one of the finest tasting oysters available. It is used, almost exclusively, for the half-shell, raw bar market.

Preparing Oysters

Before shucking, scrub the oyster with a stiff bristle brush and rinse under cool water. To shuck oysters safely you need an oyster knife. You can purchase oyster knives in almost all fish markets and in many supermarkets in the kitchen utilities sections and definitely in cookware shops. You will also need a folded kitchen towel or a metal mesh "shucking glove" to protect your hand from both the knife and the shell. These gloves are available in cookware shops and hardware stores. Never hold an oyster off a firm surface while opening it unless you are wearing a "shucking glove." Even then it's best to rest the oyster on a firm surface, such as a cutting board, and shuck. To shuck an oyster, place the oyster, bowl side down, flat side up, on a firm surface and fit the tip of the oyster knife into a crevice you'll find near the hinge. Twisting and applying pressure, push the knife firmly into the crevice and sever the hinge. Then slide the knife along the top shell and sever the adductor muscle. Remove the top shell and slide the knife under the meat to sever the bottom muscle. Clean away any bits of shell that remain and the oyster is ready.

Note: Trouble shucking oysters to serve in a Raw Bar? Place them in a freezer for five or six minutes. They'll open enough to make shucking easier. I often use a *Gilchrist Shellfish Griller* which eliminates the need for shucking and helps prevent spilling the natural juices.

Another tool for shucking oysters that works well for those of you new to shucking is the old fashioned can and bottle opener, the "church key." Fit the point of the "church key" in the space between the shells at the hinge and pry open. You will need another knife, however, to free the oyster from its shell.

Mussels

Mussels have been cultivated in France, Spain and the Netherlands for over 700 years and are important seafood throughout Europe. In the United States they were a common food of Native Americans and European settlers but somewhere along the line they fell out of favor. Still found in abundance in the cooler waters of the Atlantic and Pacific Northwest, they are the most under-utilized shellfish in the United States.

The mussel most commonly found in the wild and cultivated in the US is the *Blue Mussel*, but the imported *New Zealand Green-lipped Mussel* is gaining popularity in the US market. They are larger, meatier and overall tastier.

There are also fresh water mussels. These, I am told are editable. I have never tried them nor have I ever seen one eaten except by otters and muskrats.

The best time for harvesting mussels is from October to April because in late spring to mid-summer, they spawn and like the oyster are watery, and lean. In California, mussels are in a strict quarantine for PSP, paralytic shellfish poisoning, from May 1 to October 31. The PSP toxin, from phytoplankton Gonyaulax (red tide), accumulates in the mussel and they become unfit for human consumption. On the Pacific Coast, state officials and the growers for PSP carefully monitor commercially grown mussels. In some areas harvested mussels are put through a purification process.

Mussels, rarely eaten raw, are usually steamed, stewed, fried and grilled.

Preparing Mussels

To prepare mussels pull off the beard or byssi, the elastic and adhesive threads that allows them to attach themselves to almost a surface, with a quick tug of the hand. Scrub the mussels and rinse under cool water. They are ready to be steamed or grilled. To open raw mussels use the same method as for clams.

Conch (Whelks)

This common mollusk, pronounced *konk*, is a slow-moving, long-lived sea snail, protected by a very hard shell. This invertebrate is found in warm, shallow waters in grass beds.

Conchs, which pry open quahogs are, in turn, eaten by many animals, including rays and people. The Queen Conch, the most commonly known of the conch, is harvested for its meat and the shells used for jewelry. The Queen Conch shell can be up to one-foot long. The lip of the shell is flared with spiny ridges. The Queen Conch is severely depleted from over-harvesting and is now considered an endangered species throughout much of the Caribbean, including The Bahamas. It was once found in high numbers in the Florida Keys but, due to a collapse in conch fisheries in the 1970s, it is now illegal to commercially or recreationally harvest queen conch in that state. Therefore, the common New England Whelk is filling the bill. However, as Katie Egan, a "Conch fisherman" and researcher says: "The reality is if we don't regulate it (conch harvesting) somehow we won't be able to fish. I would not say the way it is fished now will become a problem, but it has the potential if not done properly."

Escargot (Land Snails)

Fresh snails are now available from snail farms here in the US. If they are not available in your area you may purchase them live by mail order. Gathering your own from the garden is not recommended unless you are absolutely sure that the snails you are harvesting are edible. Also there are so many pesticides used in gardens today that unless the garden is at least seven years pesticide free, (organic), why even consider it?

Preparing Escargot (Land Snails)

To prepare live snails, escargot for cooking, let them stand in 4 quarts of cold water with 1/2 cup baking soda for 24 hours. They will purge themselves. Wash them off with cold, running water and place them in an additional 4 quarts of cold water with 1 cup of white vinegar or lemon juice and 2 tablespoons salt and let them soak for 2 more hours. Rinse in fresh water for at least one hour changing the water until it is clear. Snails will come out of their shells. Discard any that do not come out of their shells. Pull off any beards. Rinse snails and shells under cold water and set aside. Melt specialty butter and fill snail shells with butter or roast garlic Aioli. Return snails to their shells and grill for 8 to 10 minutes. Be careful not to burn the shells as they are more fragile than clams. If you like you may marinate the snails in the butter or Aioli for 2 hours before grilling.

Selecting Shellfish

Fresh. That is the one word that says it all. Shellfish should be eaten as soon as possible after they are harvested. They will be eatable for up to eight days if stored properly but they are at their peak for a very brief period of time before the natural enzymes start breaking down the flesh. Shellfish, hard-shell clams, oysters and mussels, should have a tightly closed shell. If a shell is slightly open, it should close when gently tapped.

Avoid shellfish with cracked and broken shells or open shells that will not close. When purchasing steamers, touch the neck, it should shrink and try to pull back into its shell. If the neck hangs loose or the shell is open, it is dead or too far gone. Snails should pull their foot back to the shell when touched. The other important test is the "nose test." Shellfish should have a briny smell, like the sea. If you smell ammonia, an "off" odor or if there is any slime on the shells, discard. Another bit of advice is to always purchase shellfish from a reputable dealer or gather from unpolluted waters. By law, all shellfish sold to dealers, whether from a cultivator or a licensed fisherman requires a "tag" that gives pertinent information including the name of the dealer, the date and time of harvest and the area where harvested. The retailer should have this information available for you if you want it.

Storing Shellfish

Always try to purchase shellfish on the day you intend to use them. Otherwise, cover live shellfish with a damp cloth and store in the coldest section of the refrigerator but not where they will freeze. Make sure they are well ventilated. They will keep for up to seven days this way if they were fresh when you purchased them. Never put shellfish in fresh water or a closed container, they will die. If the shellfish are shucked, refrigerate in a tightly closed container.

II. THE RECIPES

Note:

Many of the following recipes call for grilling shellfish. They may be grilled directly on your grill using a *Gilchrist Shellfish Griller* or pie or pizza pans filled with rock salt to hold the shellfish upright. These methods eliminate the spilling of the juices. The shellfish may be broiled rather than grilled if you prefer.

SHELLFISH AS APPETIZERS AND SIDE DISHES

Ol' Swamper's Clams Casino

Ingredients:
24 littlenecks, prepared and unopened
24 slices Ol' Swamper's Casino Butter (page84)
1/4 cup Rolled Ritz Cracker Mix (page 107)

Preparation:
Place shucked clams on the grill. (If unshucked, grill until they open. Discard any that do not open.) Place a slice of Ol' Swamper's Casino Butter on top of opened clams, sprinkle with cracker mix, place clams under a broiler and broil until the butter bubbles and the cracker mix turns golden brown.

Serves 6

Rhode Island Clams Casino

Preparation:
Prepare clams as for Ol' Swamper's Clams Casino then sprinkle clams with a few drops of sherry and proceed as for Ol' Swamper's Clams Casino.

Traditional Clams Casino

Ingredients:
24 littlenecks, prepared and shucked
1 medium, green bell pepper, finely chopped
1/4 cup lemon juice, fresh squeezed
24 pieces bacon approximately 1" square
Salt and pepper to taste

Preparation:
Place shucked clams on the grill. (If unshucked, grill until they open. Discard any that do not open.) Sprinkle each clam with a few drops of lemon juice. Top with 1 teaspoon green bell pepper, a piece of bacon and salt and pepper to taste. Bake in preheated 400°F oven for 10 to 12 minutes or under a broiler for 3 minutes.

Serves 6

Grilled Oysters that Ol' Swamper Feller's Way

Ingredients:

24 large oysters, prepared, shucked or unopened
1 cup puréed spinach (or sorrel, watercress, arugula [rocket])
1/2 cup Rolled Ritz Cracker Mix (page 107)
1/4 lb. unsalted butter
3 medium shallots, finely chopped
2 tablespoons fresh parsley, finely chopped (page 109)
1/2 teaspoon granulated garlic
1 tablespoon Worcestershire Sauce
4 tablespoons Pernod (or Herbsaint or Anise or Galliano Liqueur)
1/4 cup shredded asiago cheese
Salt and black pepper to taste

Preparation:

Place shucked oysters on the grill. (If unshucked, grill until they open. Discard any that do not open.) Meanwhile, in a bowl, mix together spinach, cracker mixture, shallots, garlic, parsley, Worcestershire Sauce, salt and pepper. Set aside. Sprinkle Pernod over each oyster. Spoon spinach mixture onto each oyster. Top with shredded asiago. Grill until edges of oysters begin to curl and the cheese melts. This recipe goes well with hard-shell clams and mussels, too.

Serves 6

21

Oysters Rockefeller

Ingredients:
24 oysters, prepared and shucked
3 stalks scallion, finely chopped, both white and green parts
1 cup raw spinach, minced
1/2 cup plain breadcrumbs
1/2 cup Rolled Ritz Cracker Mix (page 107)
1/2 teaspoon celery salt
1 tablespoon fresh parsley flakes, finely chopped (page 109)
1/2 lb. butter
1 teaspoon Worcestershire Sauce
3 tablespoons sherry
1/2 cup grated Parmesan cheese
Salt and black pepper to taste
6 lemon wedges (page 100)

Preparation:
Place shucked oysters on the grill. (If unshucked, grill until they open. Discard any that do not open.) Combine scallion, spinach, parsley, celery salt, salt, black pepper and Worcestershire Sauce and mix well. Meanwhile, melt butter. Add butter, mixture and sherry to cracker crumbs, mix well. Place a tablespoon of the mixture over each oyster. Mix cheese and bread crumbs. Sprinkle with cheese and bread crumbs. Bake in a preheated 400°F oven for 10 minutes or until tops are golden brown. Serve with lemon wedges.

Note: Oyster Rockefellers originated, or so we're told, at Antoine's Restaurant in New Orleans and were not made with spinach. I first had Antoine's, Oysters Rockefeller in a Newport restaurant. The menu claimed that their OR's were as close to Antoine's original as anyone could get. The recipe that follows is as close to the Newport Rockefellers as we could get. ~Timothy Gilchrist

Serves 6

Almost Antoine's Original Oysters Rockefeller

Preparation:

In place of spinach in the Oysters Rockefeller recipe use 1/4 cup celery, finely chopped, 1/4 cup scallions, finely chopped, 2 tablespoons fresh tarragon leaves, finely chopped (or 1 tablespoon dried tarragon) and 1 tablespoon parsley leaves, chopped fine, (page 109). In place of the sherry substitute Pernod, eliminate the cracker crumbs, Worcestershire Sauce and cheese. Spoon mixture over oysters, drizzle with melted butter place on the grill or bake or broil as for Oysters Rockefeller.

Grilled Shellfish a la Bette Gilchrist

Ingredients:
48 littlenecks or oysters, approximately the same size, prepared, shucked or unopened
1/2 lb. Italian sausage, bulk, hot, low salt if available
1/2 cup onion, finely chopped
1/2 cup green bell peppers, finely chopped
1/2 cup red bell peppers, finely chopped
2 cups breadcrumbs, fresh
1/2 cup unsalted butter
1/2 teaspoon Worcestershire Sauce
4 tablespoons Sambuca (or similar such as Galliano or Anisette)

Preparation:
Place shucked clams or oysters on the grill. (If unshucked, grill until they open. Discard any that do not open.) Set shellfish and their liquor aside. Fry sausage until it just crumbles, drain and set aside to cool. Melt butter in a sauté pan; add onions and peppers and sauté 3 minutes. Add Worcestershire Sauce, breadcrumbs and Sambuca. Mix thoroughly. Submerge a crumble or two of the sausage in each shell and cover each of the shellfish with the breadcrumb mixture. Cook on the grill or in a preheated 425°F oven until juices begin to bubble, (approximately 3 to 5 minutes). Serve immediately.

Serves 12

Greenwich Bay Clam Company Grilled/Baked Shellfish

Ingredients:
12 littlenecks, cherrystones, top necks or oysters, prepared, shucked or unopened
1/4 cup extra virgin olive oil
1/4 teaspoon crushed red pepper flakes (optional)
3 teaspoons parsley, finely chopped (page 109)
3 cloves garlic, crushed and finely chopped

Preparation:
Place clams on the grill. (If unshucked, grill until they open. Discard any that do not open.) Combine remaining ingredients in a bowl, mix well and cook for approximately 10 to 15 minutes or until shells start to open. Place enough of the mixture on each shellfish to cover. Grill for another 5 to 10 minutes or until the liquid bubbles and the edges of the shellfish begin to curl. Serve immediately.

Note: I developed this recipe one winter while working in a Northern California restaurant. All my friends had gone to Cabo San Lucas on holiday and I had the professional chef's curse -more work than I wanted. ~Eric LeClaire

Serves 6

Grilled Shellfish Cabo San Lucas

Ingredients:
24 mussels, oysters or littlenecks, prepared and shucked or unopened
1/4 cup chipotle (smoked and roasted red jalapeños). They are available in the Mexican foods sections of most supermarkets.
3 cloves garlic, finely chopped
2 small shallots, finely chopped
1/4 cup heavy cream
1/4 cup cilantro, loosely packed, finely chopped

Preparation:
Place shellfish on the grill. (If unshucked, grill until they open. Discard any that do not open.) In a food processor, fitted with the steel blade, blend chipotles, garlic and shallots together. Slowly add heavy cream until evenly blended. Spoon chipotle-cream mixture sparingly over shellfish and grill until mixture begins to bubble. Garnish with cilantro and serve. *¡ Ay caramba! Muy caliente!*

Serves 6

Barbecued Shellfish is big a deal all over the country, not just in California. Grill 'um and enjoy 'um.

Barbecued Oysters or Littlenecks

Ingredients:
24 oysters or littlenecks, prepared and shucked or unopened
3/4 cup Tomales Bay Barbecue Sauce (page 95) or Lovely Hayawah's Korean Barbecue Sauce (page 96)

Preparation:
Place oysters or littlenecks on the grill. (If unshucked, grill until they open. Discard any that do not open.) Top with barbecue sauce to taste. Continue grilling or, if you prefer, broil until the sauce bubbles.

Serves 6

Grilled Shellfish With Ol' Swamper's Specialty Butters

Ingredients:
24 mussels, oysters or littlenecks, prepared and shucked or unopened
24 slices of your favorite Ol' Swamper's Specialty Butter (page 83)

Preparation:
Place shellfish on the grill. (If unshucked, grill until they open. Discard any that do not open.) Top with a slice of your favorite Ol' Swamper's Specialty Butter and continue grilling or, if you prefer, broil until the butter bubbles.

Serves 6

Grilled Escargot (Snails) Variation

Ingredients:
24 fresh snails

Preparation:
Prepare snails and top with your favorite Ol' Swamper's Specialty Butter. Grill fresh snails until the butter starts to bubble. Be careful not to burn the shells. Also, try snails with Ol' Swamper's Roast Garlic Aioli (page 92) or Cilantro Pesto (page 93).

Serves 6 - 8

No, this next recipe has nothing to do with Disneyland. Neither do the peppers.

Grilled Oysters and/or Littlenecks with Anaheim Chilies Salsa

Ingredients:
24 oysters or littlenecks, prepared and shucked or unopened
1-1/2 cups Anaheim Chilies Salsa (page 81)

Preparation:
Place shellfish on the grill. (If unshucked, grill until they open. Discard any that do not open.) Spoon a teaspoon of Anaheim Chilies Salsa onto each and continue grilling or, if you prefer, broil until hot. May be served with chilled oysters and littlenecks on the half shell.

Serves 6

Grilled Shellfish with Cilantro Pesto

Ingredients:
24 oysters, littlenecks or mussels, prepared and shucked or unopened
1/2 cup cilantro pesto (page 93)
1/4 cup grated dry jack or parmesan cheese
1/4 cup crumbled and buttered cornbread (page 98)
1 tablespoon unsalted butter

Preparation:
Place shellfish on the grill. (If unshucked, grill until they open. Discard any that do not open.) Meanwhile, melt butter in a sauté pan add cornbread crumbs and stir until crumbs are lightly coated. Remove from heat and set aside. When shellfish open, top with a spoonful of cilantro pesto, sprinkle with cornbread crumbs and grated cheese. Continue grilling or, if you prefer, broil until the butter bubbles or cornbread crumbs are golden brown.

Serves 6

Grilled Shellfish with Duxelles and Goat Cheese

Ingredients:
24 oysters or littlenecks, prepared and shucked or unopened
1 cup duxelles (page 91)
1/2 cup goat cheese (chèvre), crumbled

Preparation:
Place shucked oysters or clams on the grill. (If unshucked, grill until they open. Discard any that do not open.) Spoon duxelles over each. Sprinkle with crumbled goat cheese. Continue grilling or broil until cheese begins to melt.

Serves 6

We grew up in Rhode Island; an Italian heritage. There's nothing else to say about this recipe.

Grilled Shellfish with Roast Garlic Aioli

Ingredients:
24 oysters, littlenecks, or mussels, prepared and shucked or unopened
1/2 cup roast garlic Aioli (page)

Preparation:
Place oysters on the grill. (If unshucked, grill until they open. Discard any that do not open.) Spoon on roasted garlic Aioli. Continue grilling or, if you prefer, broil until the sauce begins to bubble.

Variation: purée spinach or watercress in a food processor. Spoon over shellfish. Top with duxelles and goat cheese and proceed as for above.

Note: specialty butters in your freezer provide ready toppings and sauces not only for your shellfish needs but for other foods as well. Make a variety. You will be surprised by the ease of their preparation, their versatility and popularity.

Serves 6

Grilled Oysters with Oyster Sauce

Ingredients:
24 oysters, prepared and shucked or unopened
4 large cloves garlic, finely chopped
3 medium shallots, finely chopped
2 tablespoons olive oil
2 tablespoons ginger, freshly grated **
3 tablespoons marin, saki or white wine
1/2 cup oyster sauce prepared (Available in most supermarket oriental foods sections or make per recipe page).
2 scallions, finely chopped

Preparation:
Place the oysters on the grill. (If unshucked, grill until they open. Discard any that do not open.) Meanwhile mix all ingredients, except scallion (also called, green onion or spring onion), spoon over opened oysters and continue grilling until the sauce starts to bubble and the edges of the oysters begin to curl. Garnish with sprinkling of scallion.

Serves 6

** *to peel ginger, use a spoon. It peels ginger more easily and with less wasted ginger.*

Shellfish with Three American Caviars

Ingredients:
Salmon caviar (orange or red)
Whitefish caviar (yellow)
Sturgeon caviar (black)

Preparation:
Keep caviar refrigerated until use. Keep them in their tins or glass bottles and place, half buried in a bed of ice garnished with greens or on Belgian endive. Spoon over raw oysters and clams. Add a few drops of lemon if so desired. In the summer months we use fresh grape leaves for Dolmas (Dolmas are called Diwali by the Lebanese) when we have the time. But the bottled grape leaves are good, too, and require less time and none of the cooking. Both methods are presented here. Um, Dolmas, it's Greek to us.

Mussel Dolmas

Ingredients:
24 mussels prepared and unopened
24 grape leaves (fresh or bottled)
1 cup white or brown rice, cooked
1/2 cup wild rice cooked
1 cup onion, finely chopped
1 clove garlic, crushed and finely chopped
1/4 cup parsley, finely chopped (page 109)
2 tablespoons lemon juice
1 teaspoon honey
1/2 teaspoon cinnamon
2 tablespoons extra virgin olive oil (optional)
1 large lemon sliced into thin rounds
2 cups vegetable stock
1/4 teaspoon black pepper
1 teaspoon salt

Preparation:
Place opened mussels on the grill and grill until the edges of the mussels begin to curl. (If unopened, grill until they open. Discard any that do not open.) Set mussels aside with grape leaves, lemon slices and vegetable stock. (Discard their liquor or save for future use.) In a large bowl, stir together, lemon juice, honey and cinnamon until smooth. Add rice and remaining filling ingredients.

Trim the stem off a grape leaf and place the leaf, vein side up on a flat surface. Depending on the size of the leaf place a heaping tablespoon or two of the filling and shape it into a tight little packet. Top it with a mussel. Fold the bottom of the leaf onto the filling. Fold the sides in towards the filling as far as they will go and roll towards the tip of the leaf in a firm roll, as you would as if making a burrito. Make all twenty-four and set aside.

The next step in the recipe is for both uncooked grape leaves and bottled grape leaves. In a heavy bottomed pan, or deep skillet, place a layer of lemon slices and top with a layer of 12 dolmas, fold side down. Add another layer of 12 dolmas and top with lemon slices. Place a heat resistant serving dish or spring pan bottom on top and weight it down.

This will firm up the dolmas. If you are using bottled grape leaves allow dolmas to sit this way for at least two hours in the refrigerator before serving. If, however, you are using fresh grape leaves, add the 2 cups of vegetable stock and bring to a quick boil. Lower heat, cover and simmer for ten minutes. Turn off heat and let sit, covered, for another ten minutes. Remove dolmas, allow to cool or serve warm. Just before serving dolmas, for both methods, brush lightly with olive oil if desired.

Variation: substitute oysters for mussels.

Makes 24 dolmas

This one is quick and simple and everyone we know likes Brie.

Oysters with Brie and Tricolor Bell Pepper Confetti

Ingredients:
24 oysters prepared and unopened
Brie
1 cup Tricolor Bell Pepper Confetti (page 102) for garnish

Preparation:
Place oysters on grill. (If unshucked, grill until they open. Discard any that do not open.) Slice Brie into thin slices just large enough to cover the oyster. Place on the oyster and continue grilling until cheese melts and sides of the oysters begin to curl. Garnish with confetti and serve.

Serves 6

"Swamper, do you have a good recipe for clam fritters?"
"Aeyyyuh, I do."
"May I have the recipe?"
"No suh, you cannot. I tain't no fool, you know. You'll jus' put it in a cookbook an' afore you know it, every Tom, Dick and Joseph 'ill have it."
Well, Elvira, Ol' Swamper's wife, told me he talks in his sleep. So I waited until one Sunday afternoon when he was asleep on the couch and here it is, Ol' Swamper's fritter recipe for you, me and every Tom, Dick and Joseph. ~Earl LeClaire

Ol' Swamper's "Swamp Yankee" Clam Fritters

Ingredients:
24 cherrystones or 12 quahogs prepared and unopened or shucked
2-1/2 cups all-purpose flour
1/2 cup half and half
1/2 cup milk
1/2 cup clam liquor
3 medium eggs, beaten
1 tablespoon baking powder
1/4 teaspoon baking soda
1 tablespoon grated onion
1/2 teaspoon ground nutmeg
1/8 teaspoon white pepper
1/4 teaspoon salt
Oil for deep frying (safflower preferred)

Preparation:

If unshucked, place clams on the grill until they open. (Discard any that do not open.) Rough chop clams and set aside with 1/2 cup of their liquor. Sift dry ingredients (this is important for light fritters). Slowly stir in half and half, milk, clam liquor and the eggs. Stir carefully until there are no lumps. This may be done in a food processor. Add clams and grated onion and mix well.

Drop mixture spoonful by spoonful into a deep layer of oil heated to 375°F. Put in as many as you can handle without crowding as fritters will then stick together. Cook fritters until they are brown, about a minute and a half on each side, turning once. Drain on paper towels and sprinkle lightly with salt before serving.

Serving suggestion: serve in brown paper bags, just like you get them at the beach. (Leave out the sand.) Um, umm, ummm.

"The Younger's" Conch Fritters

Ingredients:
8 conch (or 1 pound conch meat)
2-1/2 cups all-purpose flour
1/2 cup half and half
1/2 cup milk
1/2 cup bottled clam liquor
3 medium eggs, beaten
1 tablespoon baking powder
1/4 teaspoon baking soda
1 tablespoon grated onion
1/2 teaspoon ground nutmeg
1/8 teaspoon white pepper
1/4 teaspoon salt
Oil for deep frying (safflower preferred)

Preparation:
Tenderize and chop the conch then set aside. Sift dry ingredients, (this is important for light fritters.) Slowly stir in half and half, milk, clam liquor and the eggs. Stir carefully until there are no lumps. This may be done in a food processor. Add conchs and grated onion and mix well. Drop mixture spoonful by spoonful into a deep layer of oil heated to 375°F. Put in as many as you can handle without crowding as fritters will then stick together. Cook fritters until they are brown, about a minute and a half on each side, turning once. Drain on paper towels and sprinkle lightly with salt before serving.

Stuffies. Stuffies. Stuffies. When I was a kid, a feller named, Dick Brown, would often bring my parents a tray full of stuffed clams. They were always in hinged quahog shells held together with butcher's string. Those stuffies were the best I ever tasted and although he passed a recipe around, I know it's not the one he used. The sly devil. So these have to be the second best. -And they are! -EL

Stuffies (Stuffed Clams)

Ingredients:
24 medium quahogs, prepared, shucked or unopened reserve juice
and shells
3 bags of good quality stuffing, approximately 3 lb.
1lb. breadcrumbs, Italian flavored
1/2 lb. Ritz Crackers crushed to crumbs (or run through a food processor)
6 medium onions, finely chopped
3 medium green bell peppers, finely chopped
1 lb. butter (unsalted)
1-1/2 oz. whiskey (optional)
Dash Tabasco Sauce
Paprika to sprinkle
Salt and white pepper to taste.

Preparation:

If unshucked, place clams on the grill and grill until they open. (Discard any that do not open.) Rough chop clams in processor or run through a grinder. Melt butter and sauté onions and bell peppers until onions they are opaque and still firm. Add stuffing, breadcrumbs, whiskey, salt, pepper, Tabasco Sauce and mix well. Add clam juice to moisten. Wash shells and stuff with mix. Sprinkle lightly with paprika for color. Bake in preheated 325°F oven for 30 to 40 minutes. Serve hot.

Variation: Make with littlenecks or cherrystones and serve as appetizers.

Serves 12

RAW BAR

Ol' Swamper and I shucked littlenecks, cherrystones and oysters, for Raw Bars from the time we were twelve. The raw shellfish were always served on a bed of crushed ice and accompanied with cocktail sauce, lemon wedges and Tabasco Sauce. Since then we've expanded the repertoire of sauces we now include in any Raw Bar we set out. ~Earl LeClaire

Clams and/or Oysters on the Half-shell

Ingredients:
24 littlenecks and/or oysters, prepared, shucked, placed on your *Gilchrist Shellfish Griller* or grilling pan and refrigerate until being served. Serve with your favorite Raw Bar Sauce (page 77) and lemon wedges (page 100)

Serves 6

CHOWDERS, STEWS and SOUPS

This is the granddaddy of all chowders. Its simplicity is its appeal. What makes chowder a chowder rather than a soup is the addition of potatoes. It's as simple as that.

Rhode Island Clam Chowder (Clear Broth Chowder)

Ingredients:
24 quahogs (or sea clams), prepared and shucked or unopened
1 qt. clam juice, in addition to the juice from the clams
4 large potatoes, peeled and 1/2" cubed
1-1/2 medium onions, 1/4" diced
2 stalks celery, 1/4" diced
3 oz. salt pork (optional), 1/4" diced. Use 2 tablespoons canola or other plain tasting oil in lieu of salt pork if preferred.
2 cups water
1 teaspoon fresh thyme leaves chopped
1 bay leaf
Dash Tabasco sauce
Salt and white pepper, to taste

Preparation:
If unshucked, place clams on the grill until they open. (Discard any that do not open.) Rough chop quahogs or sea clams, by hand or in a processor, and set aside with their juices. In a gallon pot render all the salt pork. Add onions and celery and sauté

until onions are opaque. Meanwhile, add water to cubed potatoes and bring to a boil. Lower heat and continue to cook until potatoes are cooked through but still firm. Drain and cool potatoes under cold water. They should still be firm and set aside. Add clam juice, water, stock, thyme, bay leaves, salt and pepper to onions celery and rendered salt pork. Bring to a quick boil and remove from the heat. Before serving, add potatoes and clams and simmer for fifteen minutes or until potatoes are tender.

Serves 6 to 8

Variations:
New England Clam Chowder
Add cream or half and half to taste and thicken with a roux.

And direct to you from, where else, California...
Curried Clam Chowder
Add 3 to 4 tablespoons of curry powder to New England Clam Chowder. Adjust to taste.

We have no idea why anyone would add something that can't decide whether it's a fruit or a vegetable to perfectly good chowder in a feeble effort to take it "Uptown". But judging by the number of menus we've seen it on it confirms that old adage, "There's no accounting for taste."
Manhattan Clam Chowder
To the Traditional Rhode Island Clam Chowder add two cups of concassé (page 99) and one clove garlic, finely diced and a pinch of white pepper.

This is Not Diana from Maine's "Creamed Chili Corn Chowder with Roasted Red Peppers". This one has clams. So it is...

Not Diana from Maine's Creamed Chili Corn Chowder with Roasted Red Bell Peppers Because It Has Clams

Ingredients:
24 quahogs (or sea clams) prepared and shucked or unopened
1 qt. vegetarian stock
8 oz. frozen or fresh corn off the cob
1 roast red bell pepper, chopped, drained
1/2 pt. green chilies, chopped, drained
1/4 cup onions, diced
1/4 cup celery, diced
2 medium potatoes, peeled and 1/2" cubed
1 cup half and half
1 tablespoon butter
1/4 teaspoon fresh thyme leaves, chopped
1/8 teaspoon marjoram
1/4 teaspoon chili powder
Salt and pepper, to taste
Roux, as needed (page 98)

Preparation:

If unshucked, place clams on the grill until they open. (Discard any that do not open.) Rough chop quahogs or sea clams, set aside with their juices. In a heavy, 3 quart or gallon pot, melt butter and sauté onions and celery until onions are translucent. Combine potatoes, herb, and spices to stock and bring to a quick boil. Reduce heat and simmer until potatoes are tender. Add corn, peppers, chilies, herb and spices and heat to serving temperature. In 2 cups of the hot liquid, add roux and whisk until it thickens. Add half and half to chowder and stir in roux mixture. Stir often with a wooden spoon. Add clams and clam juices just before serving.

Note: for added flavor, grill quahogs or sea clams on your "Gilchrist Shellfish Griller" or grilling pan until they open and their liquor begins to bubble. Then chop grilled clams and use them and their juices in the chowder.

Serves 8

I made this soup one summer's day after calming in Quonochontaug Pond in Rhode Island. I had peas, snow peas and scallions in the garden, garlic and lemon in the refrigerator and a bottle of homemade, dry, white wine in the rack. ~Earl LeClaire

Grilled Clam Soup Verde

Ingredients:
24 littlenecks, prepared and unopened or shucked
1 quart clam juice
1/2 cup white wine
1 cup fresh peas
1/2 cup snow peas, minced on a bias
1/4 cup scallions, finely chopped
2 teaspoons fresh lemon juice
1 clove garlic, finely chopped
Salt and white pepper to taste
Parsley, for garnish, finely chopped (page 109)

Preparation:
If unshucked, place clams on your *Gilchrist Shellfish Griller* or grilling pan and grill until they open. Discard any that do not open. Whether shucked or grilled, set aside clams in their shells and their juices. Meanwhile, combine clam juice, wine, and lemon juice and bring to a quick boil. Add peas, snow peas scallions, grilled littlenecks in their shells and their juices. Bring to a simmer, garnish with parsley and serve piping hot.

Variation: add 1 cup of concassé, 1/4 teaspoon fresh oregano leaves, finely chopped and 1/4 teaspoon fresh thyme leaves finely chopped.

Serves 6

Ol' Swamper likes the following one. Oyster Stew, um, um, um...

Ol' Swamper's Grilled Oyster Stew

Ingredients:
24 oysters prepared and unopened
2 cups milk
2 cups cream
1/2 cup water
1/4 cup unsalted butter
1 small bay leaf
1 stalk celery finely chopped
1 scallion (green onion) finely chopped
Pinch of salt and white pepper
Six slices dry whole wheat toast, crust trimmed, cut into triangles.

Preparation:
If unshucked, place clams on the grill until they open. (Discard any that do not open.) Set aside oysters and their liquors. Meanwhile, in a saucepan or large skillet combine butter, water, oyster liquor (juice), celery, bay leaf and scallion cook over a high heat for three minutes. Slowly stir in milk stirring constantly so

milk doesn't burn. Slowly stir in cream. Remove from heat. Add oysters and return to low heat constantly stirring just until the edges of the oysters start to curl. Remove from heat and serve immediately with toast triangles.

Serves 6

Variation: for a thicker oyster stew remove 1 cup of hot liquid and whisk in roux (page 98) until liquid thickens. Whisk this liquid into the stew and heat an additional minute. Serve piping hot with toast triangles.

We came up with this recipe after oystering with "The Big Onasko" in the cold, November waters of Great Salt Pond in Point Judith, Rhode Island. "The Big O." was opening oysters as fast as he could harvest them, lacing them with chili sauce right out of a bottle and sucking them down.

The Big O's Oyster Soup

Ingredients:
24 oysters prepared and unopened
2 cups milk
2 cups cream
6 tablespoons chili sauce
4 tablespoons butter
1 teaspoon Hungarian paprika
Pinch of salt and white pepper

Preparation:
If unshucked, place oysters on the grill until they open. (Discard any that do not open.) Reserve oysters and their liquor. In a large sauce pan or double boiler, combine all ingredients except the oysters and bring to a slow boil, stirring constantly to prevent cream and milk from scorching. Add oysters and return to a slow boil. Remove from heat and serve immediately.

Serves 6

SALADS

Pushing tradition a bit here. But, after all is said and done, Rouge's Island heritage or not, I was a chef in Northern California.
~ Earl LeClaire

Salad of Grilled Shellfish with Basmati Rice, Wild Rice and Citrus

Ingredients:
16 littleneck clams, prepared and unopened
16 mussels, prepared and unopened
1 cup Basmati Rice (uncooked)
1/2 cup wild rice, (uncooked)
3 medium leeks, finely chopped, include about 1" of the green
1 large pink grapefruit, peeled and sectioned
3 cups of water
1/2 cup concassé (page 99)
1 tablespoon extra virgin olive oil
1/8 teaspoon cinnamon
1/8 teaspoon nutmeg
1/4 cup parsley, finely chopped (page 109)
Salt and coarse ground black pepper, to taste
3 cups spring mix (mixed salad greens)

Preparation:

If unshucked, place shellfish on your grill until they open. (Discard any that do not open.) Reserve littlenecks, mussels and their juices. Add shellfish juice to the 3 cups of water and, in a sauce pan, bring to a boil. Add Basmati and Wild Rice and return to the boil. Reduce heat to low, cover and continue cooking for 20 minutes or until rice is cooked. Do not remove the cover for at least 20 minutes. If rice is not done, replace cover, remove from heat and let sit for another 15 minutes. When done, let rice cool and set aside. Place olive oil in a sauté pan and sauté leeks for about five minutes. When translucent but not limp, remove from heat and add cinnamon, nutmeg and cayenne, stir for less than one minute. Add rice. Mix well. When this mixture has cooled, add shellfish, grapefruit, salt and coarse ground black pepper to taste and toss. Garnish with parsley. Serve at room temperature on a bed of spring mix.

Serves 6 to 8

Variations: Substitute risotto or orzo for rice and oranges for grapefruit. Garnish with parsley and orange or grapefruit zest.

Salad of Mussels and Gingered Spaghetti Quash with Roasted Red Peppers and Sesame Seeds

Ingredients:
36 mussels, prepared and unopened
1 medium spaghetti squash
1-1/2 cups roasted red pepper, chopped
3 cloves garlic, crushed and finely chopped
2 tablespoons fresh grated ginger (see note, page 33)
sesame seeds, toasted
1 tablespoon sesame oil
1 tablespoon lime juice
Lime zest
1 teaspoon honey
Green leaf lettuce, enough leaves to line a serving bowl, washed and spun in a salad spinner.

Preparation:
If unopened, place mussels on the grill until they open. (Discard any that do not open.) Reserve mussels. Discard liquor or save for future use. Meanwhile, split spaghetti squash in half, lengthwise, scoop out seeds and roast, skin-side up on a buttered pie plate or sheet pan in a pre-heated, moderate oven, 375°F for 30 to 40 minutes or until tender. Squash will be somewhat soft and easily pricked. Remove squash and scoop out of skin. It will come out like spaghetti. Let cool. Combine lime juice, sesame oil

and honey and whisk until well blended and smooth. Combine with all remaining ingredients and carefully toss until squash and mussels are coated with oil. Serve at room temperature or heat in microwave until just warm. Place in a bowl lined with green leaf lettuce leaves and serve.

Serves 6 to 8

Shellfish and Tortellini Salad

Ingredients:
12 mussels, prepared and unopened
12 littlenecks, prepared and unopened
12 steamers, prepared and unopened
2 lb. Cheese tortellini
1/2 cup sun-dried tomatoes, reconstituted (page 99), chopped
1 cup black olives, pitted, rough chopped
1 cup basil leaves, chiffonade, lightly packed
1/3 cup green bell peppers, ribs removed, finely chopped
1/3 cup yellow bell peppers, ribs removed, finely chopped
1/3 cup red bell peppers, ribs removed, finely chopped
2 tablespoons extra virgin olive oil
2 tablespoons garlic, finely chopped
2 tablespoons rice wine vinegar
1 teaspoon lemon juice
3 tablespoons parsley, chopped (page 109)
1 teaspoon fresh lavender flowers finely chopped, if dried, then crumble between your fingers as you add it
1/2 teaspoon of honey
Pinch of white pepper, Salt, to taste
Green leaf lettuce, enough leaves to line a serving bowl, washed and spun in a salad spinner.

Preparation:

If unshucked, place shellfish on the grill until they open. (Discard any that do not open.) Grill until the edges begin to curl.

Remove black "veil" from steamers. Set shellfish aside. (Save their liquors for future use or discard). Meanwhile cook tortellini per instructions, or add a teaspoon of oil and 1/4 teaspoon of salt in a large saucepan of water and bring to a rolling boil. Add tortellini whether frozen, dried or fresh to the water stir, bring back to the boil and reduce heat. Continue cooking until tortellini float to the surface. Remove, drain, place in a bowl of cold water and ice to "shock" (it stops the cooking and will prevent the tortellini from overcooking so that it remains, al dente). "Shock" for five or six minutes. Drain well, remove any ice and coat with just enough olive oil to coat the pasta. (This will prevent the pasta from sticking.) Add together shellfish, tortellini, bell peppers, olives, sun-dried tomatoes, basil, parsley and lavender. Combine lemon juice, vinegar, white pepper and honey. Stir together until smooth and add to the salad. Toss lightly. Chill for at least 15 minutes before serving. Just before serving toss lightly and drain off excess liquid. Place in a bowl lined with green leaf lettuce leaves and serve. The mix of the salad's colors is the garnish.

Serves 8 to 10

Conch Fritters

Ingredients:
8 conch (or 1 pound conch meat)
2-1/2 cups all-purpose flour
1/2 cup half and half
1/2 cup milk
1/2 cup bottled clam liquor
3 medium eggs, beaten
1 tablespoon baking powder
1/4 teaspoon baking soda
1 tablespoon grated onion
1/2 teaspoon ground nutmeg
1/8 teaspoon white pepper
1/4 teaspoon salt
Oil for deep frying (safflower preferred)

Preparation:
Tenderize and chop the conch then set aside. Sift dry ingredients (this is important for light fritters). Slowly stir in half and half, milk, clam liquor and the eggs. Stir carefully until there are no lumps. This may be done in a food processor. Add conchs and grated onion and mix well. Drop mixture spoonful by spoonful into a deep layer of oil heated to 375°F. Put in as many as you can handle without crowding as fritters will then stick together. Cook fritters until they are brown, about a minute and a half on each side, turning once. Drain on paper towels and sprinkle lightly with salt before serving.

"The Younger's" Conch Salad (in Rhode Islandise - Scungilli Salad)

Ingredients:
1 pound cleaned fresh conch, diced
1/4 cup fresh orange juice
2 tablespoons fresh lime juice
2 tablespoons fresh lemon juice
2 tablespoons extra-virgin olive oil
1 tablespoon chopped fresh parsley leaves (page 109)
1/2 cucumber, medium, peeled, seeded and chopped fine
1/2 yellow bell pepper, medium, chopped
1/2 red bell pepper, medium, chopped
1/4 sweet onion, medium, minced
1/2 cup tomato, seeded and chopped
1 teaspoon kosher salt
1 teaspoon fresh ground black pepper

Preparation:
Cover the conch with ice water and refrigerate for two hours. Drain and tenderize the conch with a tenderizing hammer until the meat is lacy, or use a meat tenderizer like the Jaccard Meat Tenderizer I purchased from Chefs.com. A Zyliss tenderizer also will do the job. Combine all of the ingredients, except the tomato, in a large, glass bowl. Stir and refrigerate for at least 2-4 hours to *"cook"* the conch, as you would when making *ceviche,* and to allow the flavors to meld. To serve, fold in the tomato.

MAIN DISHES

During the Great California Gold Rush and San Francisco's Heyday, oysters were a staple. One of the favorite dishes of the time was the "Hangtown Fry", an oyster omelet. When I lived in Northern Cal I use to go to Placerville to pan gold a little Southeast of there, higher in the Sierras. There's a restaurant in Placerville that serves the best Hangtown Fry we've ever had. Apparently the forty-niners didn't mind paying the outrageous prices for them as the oysters were shipped from San Francisco Bay, up the Sacramento River then hauled from Sacramento into the mountains. The Hangtown was also a favorite of the writer, Jack London, who had been both an oyster pirate and a member of the Fish Patrol (Game wardens on San Francisco Bay). London wrote a collection of short stories about his experiences with the oyster pirates, poachers and Fish Patrol, "Tales of the Fish Patrol". It's worth a read if not for the adventure then at least for the history.

P.S. They say that the chef who originated this dish was a Yankee mariner who jumped ship in San Francisco. Close enough for us.

~Earl LeClaire

The Hangtown Fry Open-faced Omelet

Ingredients:
24 oysters, prepared and unopened
3/4 cup all-purpose flour
2 eggs, beaten
10 large eggs, beaten
2 tablespoons half and half
1 cup Rolled Ritz Cracker Mix (page 107)
3 tablespoons safflower oil (as needed for frying)
1-1/2 cups stale French bread cut into 1/2 inch cubes
1/2 cup of milk
2 tablespoons unsalted butter
3 tablespoons water
1 tablespoons parsley, finely chopped
Salt and white pepper, to taste

Preparation:
Place oysters on the grill until they open and the edges of the oysters begin to curl. (Discard any that do not open.) Remove oysters and set aside. Add half and half to 2 eggs and beat well. Dust oysters in flour, coating well on all sides. Dip oyster in egg wash and roll in cracker mix. Fry in oil until golden brown and crisp. About 30 to 40 seconds on a side. Drain oysters on a paper towel and set aside. Meanwhile, preheat the broiler. Soak the French bread in 1/2 cup of milk and set aside. This is a basic panade. It adds bulk to the omelet which, when open-faced, is

much the same as a frittata. Beat together the 10 eggs and water and melt the butter in an omelet pan. Add the panade and mix well. Pour the egg and panade mixture into the pan and stir lightly until the eggs are starting to set but still loose. Add oysters and place under the broiler, keeping an eye on it at all times, until the omelet rises, is golden and set. (About two minutes.) Loosen edges from pan and slide omelet onto a serving plate. Cut into wedges as you would a pie.

Variation: for the original 'Hangtown Fry Scramble' use the smallest oysters you can find or cut medium oyster in half. Beat eggs with water and set aside. Dust oysters with flour, dip them in egg wash then roll in breadcrumbs and quickly pan fry in butter. Drain on a paper towel and set aside. Bring a well-seasoned and buttered skillet to cooking temperature and add oysters. Pour in eggs and scramble softly with the oysters until eggs are set but not dry. Spoon eggs and oysters onto plates and serve with bacon and sourdough toast.

Serves 6

This soufflé is easy enough to make but remember, it is a soufflé and requires a gentle hand and a little patience. Don't go slamming the oven door or peeking in every minute or so.

Shellfish Soufflé

Ingredients:
8 littlenecks, prepared and unopened
8 oysters, prepared and unopened
8 mussels, prepared and unopened
1 cup shellfish liquor
3 egg yolks
9 egg whites
1 cup low-fat or skim milk
2 small shallots, finely chopped
8 tablespoons all-purpose flour, sifted
2 teaspoons fresh dill, finely chopped
2 tablespoons lemon juice
1/2 teaspoon creamed horseradish
1/8 teaspoon fresh lemon thyme leaves
1/4 teaspoon nutmeg
1/4 teaspoon cream of tartar
2 cups of water
Dash salt and white pepper

Preparation:
Place shellfish the grill until they open. (Discard any that do not open.) Reserve shellfish and their juices. When shellfish cool, mince.

Meanwhile preheat oven to 400°F. Combine shellfish, lemon juice, dill, thyme nutmeg, salt and pepper and set aside. In a sauté pan sauté shallots on a low heat until they're translucent. While they cook, put sifted flour in a bowl and whisk in shellfish juices and the milk until the mixture is smooth. Put this mixture in saucepan and bring to a quick boil, whisking constantly to prevent burning. At the boil remove from heat and whisk in horseradish, then drizzle in egg yolks while whisking. Cover to keep warm.

Beat egg whites and cream of tartar in an electric mixer or hand held beaters until the whites are stiff and peak. Stir the shellfish mixture with the milk and juice mixture until well mixed. Fold about one third the egg whites into the shellfish mixture until well distributed throughout. Then fold in remaining egg whites.
Pour this mixture into a well buttered 2-1/2 to 3 quart soufflé dish (or a deep, heat-proof, loaf dish) to within a 1/2 inch of the rim. Place in preheated oven and reduce heat to 350°F. Bake for 40 minutes until the soufflé rises above the rim and the top is golden. Make sure the center has set before removing from oven. Serve immediately.

Serves 6

Rouge's Island Oyster Corn Cakes

Ingredients:
24 oysters prepared and unopened
2 cup white or yellow cornmeal (Jonnycake meal preferred)
4 eggs separated
1 cup buttermilk
1 cup skim milk
2 tablespoons molasses
2 teaspoons baking powder
1/2 teaspoon baking soda
1/2 teaspoon salt
Butter for frying

Preparation:
Place oysters on the grill until they open and the edges of the oysters begin to curl. (Discard any that do not open.) Remove oysters and cut them in half. Set aside. Discard liquor or save or freeze for later use. Meanwhile (meanwhile is a word used in recipes to mean - more work), stir together molasses and egg yolks and set aside. Beat egg whites until they peak. Combine cornmeal, butter milk, skim milk, yolk, molasses mixture, baking powder, baking soda, salt and mix well. Add oysters. Fold in egg whites, then spoon into a buttered well-seasoned skillet and fry over medium heat until golden brown. Turn and cook until the other side is golden brown as well.

Serves 6

The first Oyster Po' Boy I ever had was in New Orleans at a little place stand, which, if memory serves me, was named, "Yudda's Yummy". I was overwhelmed by the flavor or the sandwich and understood why husbands who loitered too long in the French Quarter brought them home to their wives as, la médiatrice, the peacemaker. This recipe comes from Ma Farmer's, in Pascagoula, Mississippi. Ma's was a luncheon house, which was just that, a house where five women use to cook and serve food to paying customers who dined at card tables inside the house and picnic tables outside. The food was all, of course, down home cooking and Absolutely Great! This recipe for, Oyster Loaf Sandwich, as it was called at Ma Farmer's, comes straight from Ma's mouth to mine to yours. (Oh yeah, I was told that Ma Farmer's late husband, Bert, was from Cranston, RI.) ~Earl LeClaire

The Peacemaker, (La médiatrice, or Oyster Loaf Sandwich, Oyster Po' Boy, Oyster Hero)

Ingredients:
24 oysters prepared and unopened
1 cup Ritz Cracker Mix (page 107)
1 cup all-purpose flour
2 eggs
1/2 cup half and half or evaporated milk
4 tablespoons unsalted butter, melted
Vegetable oil for frying (Safflower is my choice)
1/4 teaspoon cayenne pepper
1/2 teaspoon fresh ground black pepper

1/8 teaspoon of salt

1 -16" loaf of Italian or French bread

Po' Boy Tartar Sauce (page 105). If using a prepared tartar sauce add 1/4 teaspoon cayenne to it.

Lettuce, shredded (enough to cover the sandwich)

1 large tomato, sliced crosswise into 1/4 inch slices

Preparation:

Place oysters on the grill until they open. (Discard any that do not open.) Remove oysters as soon as they open and pat dry on paper towels. Season with salt, red and black pepper. Save the oyster liquor for future use or discard. Beat the eggs and cream together to make an egg wash. Slice bread horizontally, about 1/3 the way down from the top. Scoop out the inside of the bottom piece to form a boat-like shell, a "pirogue." Make sure, however, to leave some of the soft bread or all you'll have is a crust.

Brush the insides of the bread and place in a preheated 350°F oven 10 - 12 minutes, or until warm and crisp. Dust oysters with flour, coating well on all sides, dip in egg wash and roll in Ritz Cracker mix. Fry in oil until golden brown and crisp. About 30 to 40 seconds on a side. Drain fried oysters on a paper towel. Then assemble the Peacemaker. Spread both sides of the bread with tartar sauce, put the shredded lettuce in the bottom half and lay tomato slices along its length and put the oysters on top of it. Set the top bread on and slice crossways into equal portions. Serve immediately.

Variation: instead of putting Po' Boy Tartar Sauce on the bottom half of the loaf try it San Diego Style, with a layer of fresh avocado slices or your favorite guacamole.

Serves 4 to 6

The first time I had a bowl of, what they called, Cioppino, was in a restaurant on Columbus Ave. in "Little Italy" in San Francisco. I ordered it because it sounded familiar. When it came I exclaimed, "Oh, it's La Zuppa di Pesce! Well, alright!"

Cioppino (La Zuppa di Pesce)

Ingredients:
Onion 1 medium, chopped
Leeks 1 cup, both green and white,
Chopped garlic
3 cloves, minced
Fennel 1 cup, julienned
Tomatoes 3 cups, peeled, seeded, and chopped or Tomatoes 2 (14.5 ounce) cans undrained and chopped
Clam juice 2 (8 ounce) bottles
Bay Leaves 2
Thyme 1/8 cup fresh with stems or 1/2 teaspoon dried
Basil 2 teaspoons dried
Oregano 1/2 teaspoon dried
Parsley 1 cup fresh leaves only minced
Saffron, Mexican 1/2 teaspoon
Wine 1 cup dry red and 1 cup dry white (may red or white)
Olive oil 1/2 cup extra-virgin
Hard-shell Clams 12 (Littlenecks not Quahogs) in shell scrubbed
Mussels 12 in shell scrubbed and beards removed
Shrimp extra-large, 1-1/2 pounds raw, peeled and deveined

Bay Scallops 1-1/2 pounds

Fish Fillets 1-1/2 pounds (halibut, cod, or haddock) cut into bite-size chunks

Dungeness or Blue-shell crab meat 1-1/2 cups flaked (I leave the claws whole for cracking)

Salt and freshly ground black pepper to taste

Preparation:

In cast-iron Dutch oven or heavy bottomed soup pot or over medium-low heat, place olive oil, onions, leeks, and garlic. Cook slowly, stirring occasionally, when onions are softened add parsley, tomatoes, clam juice, bay leaves, basil, thyme, oregano, and wine. Bring just to a boil, then reduce heat to low; cover, and simmer approximately 45 minutes to 1 hour. If soup becomes too thick, thin it with more wine. Don't worry, the alcohol will boil off.

Scrub clams and mussels with a stiff brush under cold running water; remove beards from mussels. Discard any open clams or mussels. Cover with cold salted water and 1/2 cup coarse cornmeal (if you have it) let stand 5 minutes then remove the shellfish. Gently stir in the clams, mussels, shrimp, scallops, fish fillets, and crab meat to the prepared stock. Cover and simmer 5 to 7 minutes until clams and mussels open and shrimp are opaque. Do not overcook the seafood. Season with salt and pepper to taste.

Remove from heat and ladle Cioppino into large soup bowls and serve with Italian bread.

Makes 8 to 10 servings

If you want to " French" it up, serve it with a Rouille. Rouille is a garnish that consists of olive oil with breadcrumbs, garlic, and saffron. It is served with bouillabaisse and is very often used in the cuisine of Provence. They serve it with fish and plain fish soups as well.

Rouille

Ingredients
3 tablespoons water
3/4 cup coarse fresh bread crumbs (preferably from a baguette. I keep the crust on, many don't.)
3 garlic cloves
1/2 teaspoon coarse sea salt
1/2 teaspoon cayenne (optional)
3 tablespoons extra-virgin olive oil

Preparation
Pour water over bread crumbs in a bowl. Mash garlic to a paste with sea salt and cayenne. Add moistened bread crumbs and mash into garlic paste. Add oil in a slow stream, mashing and stirring vigorously with pestle until combined well. Top each bowl of Cioppino with a little of this mixture.

Pasta Primavera with Grilled Clams, Garlic, Herbs and Olive Oil

Ingredients:
24 littlenecks or 8 quahogs prepared and unopened or shucked
1 cup clam juice
1/2 cup extra virgin olive oil
1/4 cup butter
4 green onions (scallions, spring onions) chopped, white and green portions
1 cup mushrooms, sliced (we prefer maitake mushrooms, hen of the woods, available in most super markets)
8 spears asparagus blanched and sliced in half lengthways (see page 110 for blanching)
1 cup broccoli floweret's, blanched and sliced
1 small yellow or crookneck squash sliced 1/4 inch thick
4 large cloves garlic, crushed and finely chopped
1-1/2 tablespoon fresh basil leaves, finely chopped
1 tablespoon lavender, dried and crumbled fine
1/2 teaspoon fresh oregano, finely chopped
1/8 teaspoon crushed red pepper (not cayenne)
12 caper berries (large capers) rinsed well
2 tablespoons roux (page 98)
1 tablespoon parsley, finely chopped (page 109)
Dried Jack or Asiago cheese, shredded or grated

Preparation:

If unshucked, place clams on the grill until they open. (Discard any that do not open.) Chop clams, medium-fine chop, and set aside with their juice. In a sauté pan place olive oil, garlic, mushrooms, yellow squash and bring to temperature (just until the garlic starts to sizzle), reduce heat. Add clam juice, herbs and capers simmer for 3 minutes. Add roux and whisk well until sauce thickens slightly. Add clams. Serve over linguine or your favorite pasta. Garnish with Asparagus, Broccoli, shredded cheese and chopped parsley.

Variations:

(a) Add 1-1/2 cups of concassé (page 99) drained, to the sauce when adding the clams.

(b) Eliminate the roux and add 1-1/2 oz. Pernod or Anisette to the sauce. Thicken with a little Agar-Agar and water.

Serves 6

I got this recipe from the late Peter Longo, a steadfast, Portuguese shellfisherman who lived by and fished in the waters of Narragansett Bay. Peter was a great fisherman and a great cook as well. ~Timothy Gilchrist

Peter Longo's Portuguese Mussels

Ingredients:
40 mussels prepared and unopened
16 cloves of garlic, crushed and finely chopped
4 small shallots, finely chopped
1/2 cup of olive oil
2 cups concassé (page 99)
6 olives, kalamata, finely chopped
6 olives, green, sliced and finely chopped
1/2 cup basil leaves, chiffonade (narrowly sliced on a bias)
1/2 cup parsley, finely chopped (page 109)
Grilled Massa (Portuguese Sweet Bread) or Sweet Hawaiian or Potato Bread

Preparation:
Place mussels on the grill until they open. (Discard any that do not open.) Reserve mussels and their liquor. In a heavy skillet, add together the olive oil, garlic and shallots, heat until shallots turn opaque. Reduce heat and add concassé, olives, basil, mussels and their liquor. Reduce heat and simmer for five minutes. Garnish with parsley and serve hot with grilled bread.

Serves 6

SAUCES FOR A RAW BAR

Basic Cocktail Sauce

Ingredients :
1-1/2 cups chili sauce
1/2 cup ketchup
1/4 cup creamed horseradish
2 tablespoons Worcestershire Sauce
1 teaspoon lemon juice
Dash Tabasco Sauce
Salt, to taste

Preparation:
Add all ingredients, mix well in a stainless steel or glass bowl (non reactive). Serve chilled or room temperature over shellfish.

Balsamic and Shallot Sauce

Ingredients:
2 small shallots, puréed
1/4 cup tablespoons white wine
3 tablespoons balsamic vinegar
Pinch coarse ground black pepper
Pinch salt

Preparation:
In a food processor puree shallots so they are almost, but not quite, liquefied. Add remaining ingredients, mix well in a stainless steel or glass bowl (non-reactive). Serve chilled or room temperature over shellfish.

Gimlet Sauce

Ingredients:
1/4 cup Rose's Lime Juice
2 tablespoons fresh lime juice
peel of one small lime, grated
2 oz. gin

Preparation:
Combine ingredients, mix well in a stainless steel or glass bowl (non-reactive). Serve chilled or room temperature over shellfish.

Variation: for a South of the Border variation substitute tequila for gin and add a dash of salt.

Marietta's Parsley Sauce

Ingredients:
1/4 cup parsley, finely chopped (page 109)
1 clove garlic, crushed and finely chopped
1 tablespoon capers, rinsed and finely chopped
1 teaspoon lemon juice
1 teaspoon lemon peel, grated
Dash salt and black pepper

Preparation:
Combine ingredients, mix well in a stainless steel or glass bowl (non-reactive). Serve chilled or room temperature over shellfish.

Crazy Ivan's Bruschetta Sauce

Ingredients:
1-1/4 cup concassé, finely chopped (page 99)
1/8 cup parsley, finely chopped (page 109)
1/8 cup sun dried tomatoes, reconstituted (page 99)
1/8 cup celery, ribbed and finely chopped
1 tablespoon capers, rinsed, finely chopped
1 clove garlic, finely chopped
1/8 teaspoon ground anise seed
2 oz. vodka (optional)
Salt and white pepper to taste

Preparation:
In a food processor purée reconstituted sun dried tomatoes. Add remaining ingredients, mix well in a stainless steel or glass bowl (non-reactive). Serve chilled or room temperature over shellfish.

Calypso Sauce

Ingredients:
2 large, ripe mangos peeled and sliced off the seed. (Don't worry if you make a mess, it's going to be puréed).
1-1/2 oz. golden rum

Preparation:
In a food processor purée the mango and the rum together. Place in a stainless steel or glass bowl (non-reactive). Serve chilled or room temperature over shellfish.

Anaheim Chilies Salsa

Ingredients:
1-1/2 cups Concassé, diced (page 99)
3 Anaheim chilies, ribs removed, finely chopped
1/2 medium red onion, finely chopped
2 jalapeños, ribs removed, finely chopped
1/2 bunch cilantro, finely chopped
1/8 cup fresh lime juice
Salt and pepper to taste

Preparation:
Combine all ingredients refrigerate for at least a half hour.
Makes approximately 2-1/2 cups.

Todd's Grilled Clams Clam Dip

Ingredients:
24 littlenecks, prepared and unopened
1 lb. cream cheese, whipped
2 cups sour cream
2 cups yogurt
1/4 cup chives, finely chopped
1/4 cup red bell pepper, ribs removed, fine diced
3 tablespoons fresh lemon juice
1 tablespoon Worcestershire Sauce
3 tablespoons garlic, crushed finely chopped
3 tablespoons onion, finely chopped
1/2 teaspoon Dijon mustard
1/4 teaspoon salt
Parsley, finely chopped for garnish (page 109)

Preparation:
Place clams on the grill until their juices just begin to bubble. (Discard any that do not open.) Chop clams and set aside. (Save juice for future use or discard.) In a food processor whip together cream cheese, sour cream and yogurt until well blended and smooth. In a bowl, mix cream and cheese mixture with remaining ingredients. Serve garnished with parsley and your favorite crackers or toasted pita bread triangles. Makes a lot. Cut the recipe in half if you wish or do what Todd (Ol' Swamper's son, who is a professional chef) does, pipe some of the dip into Pâté à Choux.

Variation: use Todd's Clam Dip in Puffs (Pâté à Choux) (page100)

OL' SWAMPER'S SPECIALTY BUTTERS

Garlic Butter

Ingredients:
1 lb. unsalted butter, softened
2 medium heads garlic, peeled and rough chopped
2 small shallots, rough chopped
1/4 cup parsley leaves medium packed, minced
1/4 cup basil leaves, medium packed, minced
2 tablespoons lemon juice
1 tablespoon grated lemon peel
6 drops Tabasco
Dash salt
Dash white pepper
12" x 6" sheet of waxed or parchment paper

Preparation:
In a food processor, fitted with the steel blade, add garlic and shallots. Chop until they start to give up their juices. Add butter, parsley, basil. lemon juice, lemon peel and Tabasco. Blend well. Salt and pepper to taste. Blend again.

Drain off any remaining liquid and transfer mixture to a sheet of waxed or parchment paper. Shape butter into a 1-1/2" diameter log on the close edge of the paper and roll the paper around it. Twist the ends closed and chill until ready to use.

Slice rounds of butter to desired thickness, place on shellfish and grill on your Great Grate until butter melts and begins to bubble.

Variation: use roasted garlic in lieu of raw garlic (page103)

Swamper's Casino Butter

Ingredients:
1 lb. unsalted butter, softened
1/4 cup roasted green bell pepper, finely chopped (page 104)
1/4 cup roasted red bell pepper, finely chopped (page)
1/4 cup sweet onion, finely chopped (Maui, Walla Walla, etc.)
1/4 cup semi-crisp bacon, minced
1/2 teaspoon granulated garlic
1 tablespoon Pernod (may substitute Anisette)
6 drops Tabasco
6 drops Worcestershire Sauce
1/4 cup Concassé (page 99)
Salt to taste

Preparation:
In a food processor, fitted with the steel blade, add all ingredients and blend well. Drain off any remaining liquid and proceed as for Specialty Butters (see garlic butter recipe, page 83).

Olive Butter

Ingredients:
1 lb. unsalted butter, softened
1 cup black olives, pitted and chopped
1/2 cup kalamata olives, pitted and chopped
1/2 cup green olives, pitted and chopped
1/4 cup roasted red bell pepper chopped and drained (page 104)
1/4 cup roasted green bell pepper chopped and drained (page 104)
2 small shallots, chopped
1 scallion, chopped
3 tablespoons capers, rinsed and chopped
6 drops Tabasco
6 drops Worcestershire Sauce
Salt and pepper to taste
12"x6" sheet of waxed or parchment paper

Preparation:
In a food processor, fitted with the steel blade, add all ingredients and blend well. Drain off any remaining liquid and proceed as for Specialty Butters. (See garlic butter recipe, page83.)

Note: olive butter goes well with beef, too.

Lemon Butter

Ingredients:
1 lb. unsalted butter, softened
1/4 cup parsley leaves medium packed, finely chopped (page 109)
1 tablespoon fresh lemon thyme leaves, finely chopped
2 tablespoons lemon juice
3 tablespoons grated lemon peel
Salt and white pepper to taste
12"x6" sheet of waxed or parchment paper

Preparation:
Proceed as for Specialty Butters.

Wasabi Lime Butter

Ingredients:
1 lb. unsalted butter, softened
1 teaspoon wasabi paste (Japanese green horseradish)
3 tablespoons lime juice
2 teaspoons grated lime peel
1 tablespoon soy sauce
1 tablespoon marin, saki, ponzu, or white wine
12"x6" sheet of waxed or parchment paper

Preparation:
Proceed as for Specialty Butters. (Great served over fish.)

Seaweed Butter

Ingredients:
1 lb. unsalted butter, softened
1-2 sheets Nori (sushi seaweed) or Hijiki, crumbled fine
2 small shallots, fine chopped
1 tablespoon lemon juice
Dash Tabasco
Dash salt
Dash white pepper
12"x6" sheet of waxed or parchment paper

Preparation:
In a food processor, fitted with the steel blade add butter and remaining ingredients. Blend well.

Drain off any remaining liquid and transfer mixture to a sheet of waxed or parchment paper. Shape butter into a 1-1/2" diameter log on the close edge of the paper and roll the paper around it. Twist the ends closed and chill until ready to use. Slice rounds of butter to desired thickness, place on shellfish and grill until butter melts and begins to bubble.

Anchovy and Fine Herb Butter

Ingredients:
1 lb. unsalted butter, softened
8 anchovy fillets, more or less to taste (may substitute 2 tablespoons anchovy paste)
1/4 cup parsley leaves, loose pack, minced
1/4 cup watercress leaves, loose pack, minced
1/4 cup basil leaves, loose pack, minced
2 teaspoons chervil, fresh or dried
2 teaspoons fresh thyme leaves (lemon thyme preferred but is harder to get)
2 teaspoons chives, finely diced
2 tablespoons capers, rinsed, drained and rough chopped
12"x6" sheet of waxed or parchment paper

Preparation:
In a food processor, fitted with the steel blade, blend parsley, watercress, basil, chervil, thyme, chives and capers. Rough chop. Add anchovies and process until evenly mixed. Proceed as you would for garlic butter.

Butter Verde

Ingredients:
1 cup unsalted butter, softened
1/4 cup salsa verde (green salsa)
3 tablespoons Rose's Lime Juice
12"x6" sheet of waxed or parchment paper

Preparation:
Proceed as for Specialty Butters.

SUPPORTING RECIPES

Duxelles

Ingredients:
1 lb. mushrooms, white or crimini, roughly chopped
6 medium shallots, roughly chopped
2 cups white wine
1/2 lb. unsalted butter
Salt and pepper to taste

Preparation:
In a food processor, fitted with the steel blade, add shallots and blend until minced. Remove and set aside. Add mushrooms to the food processor and process until finely chopped. Remove and add to the shallots. Mix well. Meanwhile, melt the butter in a sauté pan or skillet over medium heat. Add mushroom mixture and sauté until mushrooms are limp. Add wine, salt and pepper and reduce until mixture is "moist" but not "wet".

Makes approximately 1-1/2 cups

Roast Garlic Aioli

Ingredients:
5 heads roasted garlic (page 103)
1/2 cup melted butter (may substitute extra virgin olive oil)
3 large egg yolks
3 teaspoons lemon juice
Dash Tabasco
Salt and white pepper to taste

Preparation:
To roast garlic (page 103) peel loose paper skin from garlic leaving heads intact. Place them on a sheet of aluminum foil enough to close around garlic. Wrap foil tightly and place in a pie tin. Bake in a preheated oven, 400°F, for 20 minutes or until garlic cloves are soft to the touch. Open foil, mindful of the steam, and let cool. When cool enough to handle and cool enough so they will not cook the egg, cut garlic head in half crossways and squeeze out baked garlic. In a food processor, fitted with the steel blade, add egg yolks, lemon juice, Tabasco, salt and pepper. Blend well. While blending slowly drizzle in melted butter or oil until mixture thickens enough to coat the back of a spoon. (Add butter or oil as needed.)

Variation, Quick Method: add roast garlic, lemon juice, Tabasco, salt and white pepper to prepared mayonnaise. Use a quality mayonnaise.

Makes approximately 1 cup

Yet another pesto recipe for your archives and another and another and another, ad infinitum.

Cilantro Pesto

Ingredients:
1-1/4 cup cilantro leaves, medium pack
1/2 cup parsley leaves, medium pack
4 large cloves of garlic, rough chopped
1/4 cup shallots or sweet onion, rough chopped
1/4 cup Dry Jack Cheese, grated or shredded (may substitute parmesan or asiago)
1/4 cup of toasted pine nuts (or toasted almond slivers)
1 tablespoon grated lime peel
3 tablespoons lime juice
1/2 cup extra virgin olive oil
1/2 teaspoon chili powder
1/2 teaspoon ground cumin
1/2 teaspoon salt
1/8 teaspoon white pepper

Preparation:
In a food processor, fitted with the steel blade, add shallots (or onion) and garlic. Blend for 5 seconds. Add cilantro, parsley and pine nuts (or almonds). Blend for another 5 seconds. Add the grated cheese, lime juice, lime peel, chili powder, cumin, salt, white pepper and olive oil. Blend until well mixed. All pesto freezes well.

Variations: Arugula Pesto, Basil Pesto, Sun-dried Tomato Pesto - delete the cilantro, grated lime peel, lime juice, chili and cumin from the recipe for Cilantro pesto and replace with arugula (rocket), basil or sun-dried tomatoes reconstituted, (page 99), grated lemon peel and lemon juice. Adjust salt and pepper to taste.

Makes 3 cups

Homemade Oyster Sauce

Melt butter in a sauté pan; add juice from oysters together with marin, saki or white wine, 1 tablespoon Tamari (light) (soy sauce), 1 tablespoon hoisin sauce, 1 tablespoon flour, a dash of cayenne and dash of salt. Whisk vigorously until smooth. Heat until it thickens and use in place of the prepared oyster sauce in the recipe above.

I started this barbecue sauce recipe while living within a stone's throw from the Hog Island Oyster Company at Tomales Bay, California where no self-respecting backyard get-together is complete without barbecued oysters. ~ Earl LeClaire

Tomales Bay Barbecue Sauce

Ingredients:
1-1/2 cups strong black coffee reduced to 1 cup
1 cup chili sauce
1 cup tomato ketchup
2 tablespoons red wine or cider vinegar
1/8 cup brown sugar
1/4 cup blackstrap molasses
1/4 teaspoon salt
1/2 teaspoon cayenne
1 teaspoon file`
1 tablespoon arrowroot or cornstarch
2 tablespoons water

Preparation:
Place coffee, chili sauce, ketchup, vinegar, sugar, molasses, salt, cayenne, and file` in a blender and blend until desired consistency. Pour into a saucepan and heat until it starts to bubble. Turn heat to very low and stirring, cook for another five minutes. Remove from heat and cool. Some folks like their BBQ sauce thick, others like it thin. If you desire a thicker sauce, mix

arrowroot and water. Heat existing sauce over a low flame until sauce sizzles at the edge of pan. Stirring constantly, slowly add arrowroot (or cornstarch) mixture until desired consistency is reached. Remove from heat and cool.

Makes 1 quart

Lovely Hayawah's Korean Barbecue Sauce

Lovely Hayawah? Ah yes, Lovely Hayawah. Don't you folks wish you knew the story behind this recipe? Sorry the recipe is all you get.
~ Earl LeClaire

I know the story behind this recipe and believe me it's not as interesting as "The Younger" (by three months) would lead you to believe.
~Timothy Gilchrist

Ingredients:
2 cups blue bottled plums, pits removed and plums puréed
1/2 cup hoisin sauce
1/4 cup rice wine vinegar
1/4 cup tamari (soy sauce)
1/2 teaspoon dry mustard
3 tablespoon fresh, grated ginger (see note, page 33)
1 tablespoon fresh garlic, crushed and minced
1/2 teaspoon coriander
1/4 cup chicken broth

1 tablespoon arrowroot or corn starch
2 tablespoons water
Hot chili oil to taste

Preparation:

Combine dry mustard and rice wine vinegar until mustard is smooth, add together with remaining ingredients except arrowroot, water and hot chili sauce and mix well. Place in a heavy saucepan and heat until sauce begins to bubble. If you desire a thicker sauce, combine arrowroot or cornstarch and water and stir into bubbling sauce until desired thickness is reached. Remove from heat, cool and adjust taste to desired spiciness with hot oil.

Makes 3 cups

Cornbread

Ingredients:
3 cups cornmeal, well ground
1 cup milk
1 cup half and half
3 eggs, separated
1/4 cup oil (safflower)
1/2 teaspoon baking powder
Pinch salt

Preparation:
Combine, cornmeal, milk, half and half, three egg yolks, oil and salt and mix until smooth, no lumps. Beat egg whites until they are stiff and fold in. Pour into a well-greased bread pan or larger square pan and bake in a preheated 375°F oven for 45 approximately 1 hour for bread pan and 45 minutes for square pan. Remove from oven and let cool.

Variation: soak cornmeal in milk and half and half overnight. Add 1/4 cup fresh corn kernels, 1/4 cup green bell peppers, finely diced, 1/4 cup red bell pepper, finely diced 1/2 of 1 small Jalapeño, and 1/4 cup molasses or honey.

Concassé (Peeled and Seeded Tomatoes)

Ingredients:
6 large tomatoes

Preparation:
Remove core of tomatoes with a paring knife or a tomato corer (the "Tomato Shark" is my favorite simply because of the name). On the bottom of the tomato, lightly slice an X through the skin. Place in boiling water until skins start to peel away. Remove with a slotted spoon and place in a bowl of ice water. Skins will slip away. Hold the tomato over a pan with the cored end facing down and squeeze. The seeds will fall out. Chop and store concassé until use. Tomatoes which have been peeled and seeded may be stored, covered, in the refrigerator for three or four days. Makes approximately 2 cups.

To Reconstitute Sun-dried Tomatoes

To reconstitute (soften) sun dried tomatoes, place in a heat proof bowl and pour boiling water over. Let sit for five to ten minutes and drain.

Lemon Wedges

Select firm fresh lemons. Trim off the ends. Cut into wedges and trim off pith. Make a slice in the center of the lemon wedge to the rind but not through it. When the lemon is squeezed over food it will not squirt all over the place but drop directly onto the food.

Hot Sauce (Tabasco, Crystal, Texas Pete, etc.)

Why not? If not included someone will ask for it regardless of how many other sauces you have.

Pâté à Choux

Ooh, la, la! Don't be afraid of it, all recipes sound scary in French.

Ingredients:
4 large eggs, room temperature
1 cup all-purpose flour
1 cup water
1/2 cup butter, cut into small pieces
Pinch salt

Preparation:

In a large saucepan bring the water butter and salt to a boil. Reduce heat when the butter has melted add all the flour at once while stirring with a wooden spoon. Reduce the heat to low and continue stirring until the batter pulls away from the sides of the pan. Keep stirring and beating until the batter forms a dough ball. Transfer mixture to a mixing bowl. With an electric mixer on medium-high, beat the dough until it has cooled enough so it won't cook the eggs when you add them to the mixture. When cool, add eggs, one at a time and continue beating until the egg is well mixed. The dough will go from wet and slimy to sticky to smooth with each egg. Beat in all four eggs until the batter holds a soft peak. If the dough is too stiff, beat another egg lightly and add to the dough constantly beating. The dough should fall lightly from a spoon. Don't let it get cold before piping onto cookie sheets, which have been lined with baking parchment paper or lightly greased and dusted with flour. Put dough in a pastry bag fitted with a 3/8 to 1/2 inch opening and pipe onto sheets. You may spoon the dough on as well. If tips form push them down with a moist spoon. They'll burn if you don't. Bake in a preheated 375°F oven for 25 to 30 minutes or until the puff turns golden. Test with a toothpick. It should come out almost dry. Shut off oven and continue to cook for another 10 to 15 minutes until the inside of the puff is dry. Once you take them from the oven, pierce the sides with a paring knife to let the steam escape. If not, they'll become soggy. When cooled, slice a small section off the top, fill with clam dip, put top back on and you're a cooking genius.

Tricolor Bell Pepper Confetti

Ingredients:
1 green bell pepper
1 yellow bell pepper
1 red bell pepper

Preparation:
Cut each bell pepper lengthwise in four quarters, from the stem to the tapered end, without cutting into the seed pod that hangs from the stem. Trim the pepper from the stem end and the rounded bottom of the pepper. Set aside for use elsewhere. Remove the white ribs from the inside of the pepper and discard. Lay the pepper, skin side down on a flat surface and, as if removing the skin from a fish fillet, run the blade of a sharp knife along the length of the pepper removing about half the thickness of the fleshy part of the pepper. Save it with the trimmed pepper pieces for future use. Slice the pepper lengthwise into thin strips. Keeping the lengths of pepper together as a bundle turn sideways and slice, on a bias, to about the size of confetti. Mix the peppers together and use as a garnish.

To Roast Garlic

Method 1:

Remove loose "paper" from whole garlic heads. Place heads in pie pan, sprinkle with oil, salt and black pepper. Cover tightly with aluminum foil and bake at 400° for 30 minutes, or until garlic is soft. Remove garlic and squeeze individual cloves or slice heads in half to expose half of each clove. May remove exposed garlic or, if serving with brie or with bread as appetizer, leave and serve in halves.

Method 2:

Place whole cloves of garlic in heavy sauce pan with enough olive oil to cover and heat until olive oil starts to bubble. Remove from heat and cover let sit 30 minutes or until olive oil has cooled. Strain off olive oil and save for future use as garlic flavored olive oil. Drain garlic on paper towels. Squeeze each clove to get "roasted" garlic.

To Roast Bell Peppers

Ingredients:
Red bell peppers
Green bell peppers
Yellow bell peppers

Preparation:
Grill peppers on your *Gilchrist Shellfish Griller*, gas stove burner or in an oven until the skins of the peppers blister and char. Turn with tongs until peppers are blackened. Place blackened peppers in a paper bag** and twist or fold mouth of bag closed. This will allow the steam to separate the skin from the flesh of the peppers. Place the bag in a tray to catch any liquid that drains through. Let peppers sit for twenty minutes. When the when they are ready, place in a bowl of ice water and skins will fall away. Remove stems and seeds. Slice peppers and trim away white ribs. Chop and continue to drain in a colander or strainer.

Makes approximately 2 cups

Roast peppers may be stored, covered, in the refrigerator for three or four days.

**plastic bags may be used in place of paper but I prefer paper bags. Plastic will, on occasion, melt and often gives off chemicals which affect the taste and safety of the product.

Po' Boy Tartar Sauce

Ingredients:
3 egg yolks
1 cup olive oil (or as needed)
1 tablespoon hot water
1/2 cup scallions, finely diced
1/4 cup parsley, finely chopped (page 109)
1/4 cup dill pickle, finely chopped and drained
1/2 teaspoon Dijon mustard
1/4 teaspoon cayenne pepper
1/2 teaspoon lemon juice
1/4 teaspoon salt

Preparation:
Put egg yolks, mustard, cayenne, lemon juice and salt in a food processor fitted with a steel blade and blend on a low setting. With motor still running drizzle the oil in through the feed tube until the mayonnaise thickens. Blend in the water. Adjust seasonings to taste. Remove to a bowl, add scallions and pickles and mix until evenly dispersed throughout.

Grilled Massa (Portuguese Sweet Bread), Hawaiian Sweet Bread, or Potato Bread

Ingredients:
One loaf of Massa, Hawaiian Sweet Bread, or Potato Bread sliced in half, horizontally
1/4 cup unsalted butter, melted
1/8 cup extra virgin olive oil
1/4 teaspoon salt
1/4 teaspoon oregano
Paprika

Preparation:
Brush butter and olive oil on both sides of bread. Sprinkle on salt, oregano and paprika. Grill, butter side down, (or place under a closely watched broiler), until bread is golden brown and crisp. Don't leave it. Once it reaches a certain point it will burn quicker than you can get it off the grill or out from under the broiler.

Serves 8

We've tried all the crackers and Ritz is still our favorite for this recipe. My mother, Ginny, makes a great "Mock Apple Pie" with Ritz crackers. Maybe that is why I am so fond of Ritz. ~Timothy Gilchrist

Ritz Cracker Mix

Ingredients:
1 lb. Original Ritz Crackers
1/2 lb. unsalted butter, melted
1/4 cup parsley leaves loosely pack, finely chopped
1-1/2 oz. Pernod (may substitute anisette or sherry)
1 teaspoon thyme leaves, chopped (lemon thyme preferred)
2 teaspoons granulated garlic
2 teaspoons onion powder
1 teaspoon paprika
2 tablespoons Worcestershire Sauce
1 teaspoon Tabasco Sauce
Salt and white pepper to taste

Preparation:
Put crackers in plastic wrap, plastic bag, or wax paper, place on a board and with a rolling pin, or the bottom of a skillet, crush crackers to breadcrumb consistency. Place in a large mixing bowl. Add remaining ingredients and mix well by rubbing mixture between the palms of your hands. The Ritz Cracker mixture may then be spread out on a sheet pan to air dry for an hour and placed in a bowl, covered and stored in a dry, cool place until use.

Makes approximately 1 quart

Roux

Ingredients:
2 lb. Butter or margarine (Margarine? Heave, heave. Yeah, we know, Dr. Doctor, we know that you said, "No butter!" But sometimes a cook has to be true to the craft and ignore the Good Physician's warning. Life is a matter of compromise. If you feel you must use margarine, then by all means, go ahead. Who are we to pull the mask off the Lone Ranger?)
2 lb. all-purpose flour

Preparation:
Melt butter or margarine in a large skillet and slowly add flour constantly stirring. Consistency should be like loose pudding, Keep stirring while over heat until it is somewhat dryer and is light brown in color and nutty in flavor. Remove from heat. You may use what you want and place the remaining roux in a stainless steel bowl, cover with plastic wrap and leave at room temperature for three days. (It will keep in the refrigerator for up to a week.)

A number of years back, I worked as chef saucier for a Swiss-born, French-trained chef who'd started out as a line cook at the age of ten. He was a man who still believed in servitude. One busy night I was garnishing the plates and passing them through the chef's window to the wait staff. I'd add a strategically placed Johnny Jump Up and a touch of parsley for garnish before handing the dish off. I was sprinkling parsley on one plate when suddenly, Whack! The flat of a metal spatula slapped the back of my hand so hard it left a welt. Chef René, spatula in hand, stood there shouting in his Swiss-French-American accent, "Don't you know how to parsley a plate? Where did you go to school, in Rhode Island? " Well, I've never forgotten that rebuke and when the kitchen closed for the evening, Chef René and I had a serious talk about the improper use of metal spatulas and the advantages of having of Earl The Younger's having been raised in Little Rhody. I bet he hasn't forgotten that little lesson in courtesy, and "Rouge's Island" justice.
~Earl LeClaire

Chopped Parsley or Cilantro for Garnish

Preparation:
1 bunch parsley or cilantro, just the leaves, discard main stems. Finely chop leaves and place in a clean cloth. Close cloth around parsley or cilantro and rinse with cold water. Squeeze water out. It will run green with chlorophyll. Continue rinsing until water runs clear. Turn parsley or cilantro out into a bowl. This method will keep parsley or cilantro fresh longer and is easier to use for garnishing.

Blanching

Blanching is a simple cooking technique whereby you briefly put food (usually vegetables) into boiling water for 1 to 4 minutes then "shocking" them by plunging the food immediately into an "ice bath", a water bath with ice cubes in it, to stop the cooking process. Blanching helps food retain its vibrant color and distinct flavor. It is best to plunge the food into the boiling water using a wooden handled strainer. This eliminates "fishing" in boiling water to remove it or simply drain the hot water and blanched food into a strainer then plunge into the "ice bath". This method is also used to remove skins and peels from fruits and vegetables (see Concassé, page 99).

III. THE TRADITIONAL NEW ENGLAND CLAMBAKE

Growing up in Rhode Island, a summer without a clambake would have been like a Thanksgiving without a turkey. We never knew a summer without three or four bakes. Clam chowder, lobsters, steamed clams, stuffed clams, littlenecks on the half shell, flounder wrapped around a pork sausage, baked scrod, baked white potatoes, sweet potatoes, onions, corn on the cob and Indian pudding. Um, umm, ummm. Dining ecstasy beyond compare.

During the summer my parents catered clambakes for company picnics and family reunions. Not only did Ol' Swamper and I help supply the bakes, (we dug clams, hauled lobster pots and filleted fish), but we worked them. We ran errands, (yeah, gofers, that was us), for the "Bakemaster" - ruler absolute of the event, gathering rocks, seaweed and, depending upon the time of day, fetching coffee-one cream, no sugar, or a bottle of ice-cold beer. We also "prepped" food, shucked clams and helped dish out the meal. But the best part of working the bakes was when, after everyone had been served, Ol' Swamper and I got to help ourselves. We'd take our bowls of chowder and plates, piled high with, lobster, clams, drawn butter, fish and all the rest, including a beer if we could get away with it, to a picnic table that had been placed in the shade of a tree far from the merry crowd, sit with coworkers to laugh, talk and feast on the greatest of all shore dinners.

~Earl LeClaire

*There are two types of clambakes, the "pit bake" which requires more preparation and work than the other but is the **classic** bake and the now more common 'barrel bake' which is easier and almost fail-safe. Now these are **traditional** Rhode Island "Little Rhody" clambakes we're talking about here. No roasted corn with chipotle butter, soft-shelled clams steamed in wine with assorted herbal infusions, or littlenecks on the half shell with a balsamic vinegar, caper and shallot sauce, regardless of how good they are. If you want to embellish or create your own tradition go right ahead, but our purpose here is to try to record a bit of American, gastronomic history. Called **Appanaug** (app´-a-nawg), the Algonquian word meaning "seafood cooking" clambakes were first held by the Indians of New England to celebrate abundant harvests, the change of seasons or to honor an individual for contributions to the tribe. This custom continues today among the Wampanaugs of Massachusetts and the Narragansetts of Rhode Island. As Europeans began to populate the "New World" they adopted and adapted much of the Amerindian cuisine. Clambakes, appanaug, fast became a summer tradition.*

The Pit Bake

To prepare a 'pit bake' for twenty-five people you will need a pit, one foot deep and three feet in diameter; enough dry, igneous rocks, eight to ten inches in diameter, to fill the pit, a wire mesh to fit over the pit, desirable but not essential (chain-link fence or barbecue grills work), firewood and tinder, rockweed (Fucus), a wet canvas to cover the pit and keep the steam in, (a plastic tarp or wet burlap will suffice), and enough food to feed twenty-five. The food should be prepared ahead of time as directed and kept refrigerated (or iced down), until ready for use. Remember, seafood spoils quickly in heat. You will also need a large baking potato which is the Bakemaster's "test potato".

The "Bakemaster" may assign specific tasks to members of the group to make the bake a group effort. First, dig the pit. Meanwhile, find the igneous rocks. (Wet, porous rocks are dangerous because they may "explode "when heated). Gather the kindling and firewood. Seasoned hardwood burns hotter. You may substitute charcoal for the wood if need be. Harvest the seaweed, enough to cover the pit twice and soak in seawater or potable water. Place the tinder and wood (or charcoal) on top of the rocks and allow it to burn until it is white-hot about two to three hours. When the embers are ready, spread them over the rocks with a shovel or rake, allowing them to fall between the cracks to help heat the rocks more evenly. Add more wood where needed. Always being mindful of the possibility of exploding rocks. Finally, when the embers die down, sweep the residual ash off the rocks and lay the wire mesh over. Now you are ready to bake. Here speed is essential. Put down a layer of rockweed. It will start to steam immediately. Arrange the food as shown in *Figure 1*. Place the "test potato" on top of it all. Add another layer of rockweed and cover the bake area with the canvas, tarp or burlap. Anchor the edges with large rocks or planks to keep the steam in. The aroma will fill the air and whet appetites. Now the vigil must be kept. Let it steam for about an hour or until the 'test potato' is cooked through. Then, if you are the "Bakemaster," the person upon whom will be bestowed incredible praise if the bake has gone well or piteous scorn if the food is scorched, cross your fingers, hold your breath, be anxious, uncover the bake, remove the food and serve it up with chowder, "stuffies" and drawn butter.

The Barrel Bake

The "barrel bake" is a more practical and convenient way of preparing clambakes especially for backyards and public picnic areas. For a bake that will serve twenty-five people you'll need an open, sturdy barbecue grill, charcoal or wood, a thirty to forty gallon galvanized trash can or stock pot with a lid, water, a wooden or metal rack that will fit in the bottom of the barrel or pot, seaweed and the food. See *Figure 2*.

To insure proper cooking, it is important not to let all the water evaporate. To be safe, we add two quarts of water when the bake has been underway for thirty minutes.

PIT BAKE

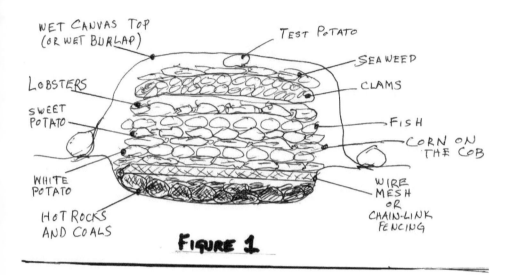

WET CANVAS TOP (OR WET BURLAP)

TEST POTATO

SEAWEED

CLAMS

LOBSTERS

SWEET POTATO

FISH

CORN ON THE COB

WHITE POTATO

WIRE MESH OR CHAIN-LINK FENCING

HOT ROCKS AND COALS

FIGURE 1

BARREL BAKE

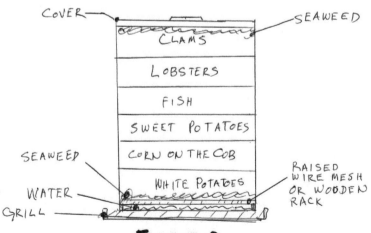

COVER

SEAWEED

CLAMS

LOBSTERS

FISH

SWEET POTATOES

CORN ON THE COB

WHITE POTATOES

SEAWEED

WATER

GRILL

RAISED WIRE MESH OR WOODEN RACK

FIGURE 2

115

The Clambake Recipes

Clambakes may be held on the beach, in backyards, picnic groves, or anywhere else where outings can be held. "Pit bakes" however, when held in public spaces often require permits and approval issued by local authorities and fire departments.

These recipes serve 25 people.

Rhode Island Clam Chowder (a clear broth chowder)

Prepare enough to serve twenty-five.

Raw Bar: Littlenecks and/or Oysters on the Half-shell for 25

Ingredients:
Littlenecks or oysters, shucked and refrigerated or iced for twenty-five people. (Allow for six shellfish apiece, minimum. You know your guests better than we do. We only wish we could get away with a minimum of six apiece but our friends are shellfish gluttons.)
Lemon Wedges (page 100)
Cocktail Sauce (page 77)
Additional Raw Bar Sauces to suit. (page 77)
Serve hot with a dribble of heavy cream.

Lobsters

Ingredients:
25 live East Coast lobsters (Maine Lobsters)

Note: keep lobsters refrigerated or on ice with wet seaweed. Make sure all claws are banded or pegged.

Steamed Clams

Ingredients:
1 peck soft-shelled clams, preferably steamers

Note: place steamers in bags and keep refrigerated until use.

Drawn Butter (for steamers, lobsters, mussels, etc.)

Ingredients:
2 lbs. sweet Butter
1/2 sprig fresh thyme
2 teaspoons lemon juice
Dash white pepper

Preparation:
In a saucepan melt butter. Add thyme, lemon juice and white pepper. Serve warm.

Stuffies (Stuffed Clams)

See recipe, page 41, and make enough for twenty-five guests.

Clambake Flounder and Sausage

Ingredients:
25 fillets flounder, medium to large
25 links pork sausage, precooked
salt and pepper, to taste
25 tabs butter

Preparation:
Wrap each fillet around a pork sausage. Sprinkle with salt and pepper to taste. Top with a tab of butter. Wrap each fillet in aluminum foil. Refrigerate until use. Place the 25 wrapped fillets in cloth bag or place all in a cheese cloth and tie up as a bag. (Cheap, new pillowcases work well as cloth bags for the bake.)

Baked Scrod (Codfish)

Ingredients:
25 pieces scrod, approximately 4 oz. each
2 cups Rolled Ritz Cracker Mix (page 107)
1 cup white wine, (more if needed)
25 tabs butter
Salt and pepper, to taste

Preparation:
Place scrod in aluminum foil. Sprinkle with white wine. Cover lightly with cracker crumbs and top with butter tab, Salt and pepper. Fold aluminum foil to cover and seal. Place all scrod in bags as with flounder. Refrigerate until use.

White Potatoes

Ingredients:
25 medium white potatoes, bakers, scrubbed, skin on
Bacon drippings or vegetable oil, as needed

Preparation:
Scrub potatoes; rub lightly with bacon drippings or vegetable oil. Wrap in aluminum foil. Bag, as with fish. Store at room temperature until ready to use.

Sweet Potatoes

Ingredients:
25 medium sweet potatoes, scrubbed, skin on
Bacon drippings or vegetable oil as needed

Preparation:
Treat the same as white potatoes.

Corn On the Cob

Ingredients:
25 ears fresh corn

Preparation:
Peel back the outer husks, remove the inner husks and the silk and return husks to cover the ear. Soak in cold water for an hour then bag as with potatoes.

Indian Pudding

Ingredients:
1 gal milk, scalded
4-1/2 cups yellow cornmeal
9 tablespoons butter
2 cups molasses

1 cup brown sugar, light
6 large eggs, beaten
2 cups raisins, yellow seedless preferred
1 cup currents
2 teaspoons ground allspice
2 teaspoons ground ginger
1 teaspoon ground nutmeg
2 teaspoons baking powder
1/4 teaspoon baking soda
Salt, pinch
1 qt. heavy cream

Preparation:
Bring 3-1/2 quarts of the milk to a boil (scald), and place it in a double boiler. Slowly add the cornmeal stirring constantly with a wooden spoon or stainless steel wire whip. Stir in salt and butter. Cook over a low heat, stirring often, for fifteen minutes. Stir in the molasses, sugar and eggs. Add raisins, currents and spices. Meanwhile blend the remaining 1/2-quart of the milk with the baking powder and soda. Stir it into the pudding mixture. Pour the mixture into lightly buttered casserole dishes (to six quarts). Be careful not to splash mixture onto the sides of the dishes as the spilled pudding will burn. Bake in a slow preheated oven (250° -275°) for 2-1/2 to 3 hours or until a dry butter knife comes out clean and pudding is firm. Serve with vanilla ice cream. The pudding will go farther and it is a traditional topping. May also be served with whipped cream if preferred.

IV. APPENDIX

Units of Measure Equivalents

3 teaspoons	1 tablespoon
4 tablespoons	1/4 cup
8 tablespoons	1/2 cup
12 tablespoons	3/4 cup
16 tablespoons	1 cup
2 cups	1 pint
4 cups	1 quart
4 quarts	1 gallon
8 quarts	1 peck
4 pecks	1 bushel
1 liquid ounce	2 tablespoons
8 liquid ounces	1 cup
32 liquid ounces	1 quart
16 ounces	1 pound
pinch	1/8 teaspoon or less
dash	4 drops to 1/4 teaspoon

Bibliography

Shellfish and Seaweed Harvests of Puget Sound (Washington Sea Grant Publication) - Daniel P. Cheney, Thomas F. Mumford, 1986

National Sea Grant Research Program: Report on Marine Biotechnology, 2000

Reuters University, www.hsrlrutgers.edu, 2001

Where to Get It

(Gilchrist's Shellfish Griller) GreatGrates are being used in homes, restaurants and catering companies due to their simple, versatile, and functional, time tested design. While *Great Grates* are often used to cook unopened shellfish, many chefs also use them for cooking and serving previously opened clams, oysters, quahogs and mussels. Experience delicious clams casino, stuffies, oysters Rockefeller, mussels in garlic butter with all the juices and seasoning in each shell made possible without rock-salt and excessive, time consuming handling. *www.greatgrate.com*

Watch Hill's®Oysters (East Coast)
Jeff Gardner, Aqua culturist
Farm Raised Oysters and Littlenecks
Raised in the pristine, tidal waters of Rhode Island's Winnapaug Pond
Rated as the best tasting oysters in America by Gourmet magazine
www.farmfresh.org/food/farm.php?farm=775

Ninigret Oyster Farm (East Coast)
Oysters, Quahogs, Scallops, Steamers
Ninigret Oyster Farm is a 1 acre farm run by Robert Krause
Post Rd. and Wildflower Rd.
Charlestown, RI
Phone: (401) 529-3519 preferred
ninigretoysters@verizon.net

Taylor Shellfish Farms (West Coast)
Oysters, Clams, Mussels and Geoduck
From Western Washington State's Puget Sound
A state of the art farm with over a century of experience combined
with modern technology
www.taylorshellfishfarms.com

Recipe Index